First published 2015

© 2015 Vinita Ramtri

ISBN-13: 978-1518871580
ISBN-10: 1518871585

VR BOOKS is the imprint under which Vinita Ramtri's
work not intended for other publishers
will henceforth appear.

'After all the focus on remediation and stopping people doing bad things, it's great to see a book focused on how we now move on to using conduct positively to make the right proactive decisions in building great businesses that deliver better outcomes for clients. Supporting businesses and people that do the right things must be the right objective for all of us.' **Pete Horrell, ex-CEO, Barclays Wealth**

'Conduct risk is becoming more and more a buzz word in the financial industry and for regulators. Amidst today's evolving operating landscape, Vinita has been instrumental in helping senior leaders and colleagues at Barclays interpret and make sense of what good conduct risk management entails, all with a focus on making a tangible difference for our clients, colleagues and the wider industry. Converting theory into practical implementation advice, Vinita has provided pragmatic support and direction to the business, enabling each region to evolve conduct journeys tailor-made to meet their own set of priorities. Through this book, she shares her insights and experience, bringing to readers many practical examples that they can identify with and think through for their own businesses. This is definitely a worthwhile read not just for banking practitioners but for professionals looking at conduct risk management across all industries.' **Didier Vondaeniken, Head of Barclays Wealth, Asia Pacific**

'Jonathan sighed. The price of being misunderstood, he thought. They call you devil or they call you God.'

Richard Bach, *Jonathan Livingston Seagull*

*

'Humans are odd; they think order and chaos are somewhat opposite.'

Avengers: Age of Ultron

Contents

Where I stand

I'm walking along a road. It's busy out there. I want to cross. I stand and stare. I stand at the side and look like I have a purpose. I am interested in getting to the other side.

People see purpose. Someone eventually stops and lets me cross. Sometimes, that's all it takes to get to the other side, a sense of purpose and the conviction to follow through – ten steps to the other side of the road or the thousands of words to the last page of this book.

My story is about conduct and ethics. The *Oxford English Dictionary* defines conduct as the manner in which a person behaves, especially in a particular place or situation. In the post-crisis world, it refers to the behaviour of banks in the context of their customers and the economy at large.

My story, however, is not about the conduct of my bank or yours, my country or yours – it is about our world. Not the world of yesterday or tomorrow, but the world as it always has been and always will be.

The book offers a general insight into why we feel it is okay to dislike banks and bankers, but it also questions if the rest of us are any different. Using conduct as the main theme, I seek to understand how we operate the way we do in organisations, at home, as employees, parents, leaders and even children. I also look at what makes us behave the way we do and explore the contradiction between our outwardly non-acceptance of behaviour that we ourselves may be demonstrating.

Is the man in the arena different from the spectator, the doer different from the done, or are they two sides of the same coin? Often in our endeavor to resolve issues, we lose sight of the problem and solutions consume us. Good conduct is a concept introduced to ensure that we do what is right by people and society, and it is often hailed as the new mantra, the Holy Grail, the answer to everything that went wrong. The story started with traumatised customers: men, women and families who lost life savings and whose homes got repossessed as the crisis unfolded.

However, as debates and discussions seem more focused on firms, regulators, fines, leadership, data, consultants, politics and politicians, I wonder who's tuning into the people, and to whom they are looking for answers?

I wonder if this phenomenon of losing sight of the goal is limited to the financial world or whether it is an extension of who we are. In our desire to earn more for our children, do we forget how critical it is that we spend time with them? In our pursuit of a happy life, do we forget to stop and smile at the many happy moments that life has to offer? In our desire to seek true love, don't we sometimes drive it away? As we constantly chase control over solutions, do we lose sight of the problem we were trying to solve?

I also explore what people make of the behavioural clean-up. Do they believe that banks are trying hard to change their behaviour, and do they even care anymore, or does all of the activity just fade into background noise as they drift from one headline to the next? When they read of the high-profile fines and hear about banks being punished for bad behaviour, do they feel vindicated, deriving a sense of justice, or do they grow yet more concerned, wondering whom they can trust?

Finally, as papers report one big fine after another, what does this do to an organisation, its culture and its people? How does it impact their morale? Is it that everyone, in all firms, needs to correct their behaviour? And, if yes, is there a right and a wrong way to do so? Does this constant battering come at a cost? If so, what is that cost?

So come on, let's tune in.

Introduction

The aftermath of the financial crisis, which started in 2008 and continues even today, has left a burning need for banks and financial institutions to clean up their act. The reputation of banks has hit rock bottom and there is much to redeem. Large fines imposed by regulators worldwide and the high cost of putting things right have ensured that the issue has been at the forefront of media attention and public debate.

There is clearly a problem that needs to be solved. In this book, I look at the breadth of the issues and ask: if banks are the most popular rogues of the day and we all love to hate them, are the concerns limited only to them or are they symbolic of a general social degradation?

Fixing core issues comes with its own challenges. In a rushed effort to get things right, and a burning desire never to err again, might we be creating more problems? As we shame the industry into correcting its mistakes, do we believe that it is possible to be right all the time?

The book explores whether, in our constant focus on fixing bad behaviour at banks, we are tipping from one extreme to the other. Is there any such thing as the right balance or is that a golden truth that will forever elude us?

*

'So have you embedded conduct yet?' a friendly voice called out to me as I headed to the office gym. Often referred to as the 'conduct girl', my name is synonymous with conduct. When people ask what book I am writing, they add, 'Don't tell me it's about conduct.'

Yes, the book is about conduct. It is about conduct and everything else, because, like life, conduct on its own has no meaning. When we write about life, we need to capture memories, thoughts, and conversations – moments stolen and moments seized. In the same way, when we write about conduct, we need to capture context, rationale, decisions and impact. Everything in life, including conduct, is about the synthesis of various facets and how they evolve in relation to one another. It's all about culmination.

We get out of bed in the morning to do something we feel passionate about and to do it well. We don't wake up purely to conduct ourselves well. Doing something ethically or not is always in relation to a primary purpose and is not a purpose in its own right. Conduct and ethics are therefore a large part of this book in that they form the backdrop that is often used to classify decisions as good or bad.

What I mean by conduct is simply the way we conduct ourselves. Hidden beneath that simple definition is a certain depth, because it encapsulates our understanding of situations, the judgement that we exercise in making decisions, the messages we communicate, the behaviours that we display, the impact of these behaviours, and everything else in between. Conduct can be seen as a value, such as organisations' desire to uphold high standards, or it can be seen as the risk of making decisions that may harm people. It may be seen as something for which leaders should be responsible, or something that every individual should bear in mind. Given the breadth of situations that can be associated with this word, it is no surprise that the industry struggles with definitions and taxonomy. Depending on who you talk to, you find variations in people's understanding of conduct and its role in financial services today.

Throughout this book, I have approached our efforts to restore good conduct in banks and related discussions from different angles, sharing thoughts and reflections as seen through the eyes of an employee, a customer, a parent and a leader. As we try to resolve issues in our own ways, I note that the one thing we lack is the common denominator. My hope is for this book to provide just that. The story could be a pocket guide for leaders, managers and keen customers wanting to dig deeper into the interesting evolution of conduct in the post-crisis era.

Much of this book is set in the UK, yet the principles can be applied worldwide. As the saying goes, a butterfly flapping its wings in New Mexico has the power to cause a hurricane in China. In 2008, the crisis that started in the US[1] made its way to China; in 2015, as all eyes were on the Chinese Yuan and even the South China Sea, it would be prudent to accept that we are more interconnected than we may care to admit.

This book is a simple collection of life. Simply because, if we need to correct something that applies to society at large, then society needs to be part of the correction just as much as firms and regulators. I have used several day-to-day stories, conversations and reflections, not with the intention of attacking anyone but to illustrate my point in the simplest possible way.

The conduct debate is fast-moving history; each day brings new observations, new regulations and new positions. Yet lessons on conduct are not new to any of us. Hindu mythology covers extensive discussions of conduct in *Mahabharata*,[2] the epic narrative of

---

[1] See chapter, The financial crisis.
[2] One of the two major Sanskrit epics of ancient India.

the Kurukshetra war. Conduct principles are universal and can be applied to my grandparents and my children alike. Examples used in this book may correspond to different times and places, but it is the principles that we need to elicit through the stories.

I'm often asked for solutions, checklists, the silver lining, the project plan to fix all things conduct, and here my aim is not to give you a list of list of answers, but guidelines to help you seek thoughts about the wrongs and rights of and better understand what you discover. We will touch upon some tools and concepts but, more importantly, I hope to be able to offer insight and perspective so you can apply them in the context of your environment.

Conduct, in my view, has less to do with answers and more with asking the right questions – of ourselves and of others. I hope, therefore, that I am able to get you to stop and think, and to go away from this book with a desire to ask.

This world does not come with a process manual and never will. Often the answers come before the questions, which is precisely the reason we need to tune in and pick up the beat.

I urge you to mix my views with your reality, recognising the events surrounding you that caused you to pick up this book and the reason why you and

I are connected at this precise moment. Answers will then emerge from within.

This book is for those who seek to understand and are not afraid of asking questions. And definitely, for those who are not afraid of making mistakes.

'There cannot be a crisis next week. My schedule is already full.'

Henry A. Kissinger

1. The financial crisis

I remember quite clearly one September morning in 2008. It was a sunny day in Scotland as I drove to work. Just as I hit the M8, the radio news announced that Lehman Brothers had gone bankrupt. It sounded catastrophic, but frankly I had no clue what it meant in real terms.

Little did I know that this was the beginning of a financial crisis that was going to engulf economies, haunting us for years to come. What started with the collapse of Lehman Brothers (one of America's largest banks) almost brought down the world's financial system. The news was all over the papers, and was nothing short of mindboggling. The crisis brought markets to the brink of collapse and toppled share prices, wiping out tens of trillions of dollars. It obliterated the retirement savings of millions and crippled economies.

The crash finds its roots in the US subprime lending – which essentially meant that a significant amount of loans had been made available to those who would have difficulty in meeting the repayment requirements. The loans defaulted, eventually resulting in sharply declining home prices, with large numbers of customers losing their savings and their homes. It had taken over a year for events to unfold to the point when Lehman Brothers collapsed. Questions had been asked and issues raised, but perhaps this was how it was meant to unfold. People had assumed that governments would always step in to bail out a bank that got into serious trouble – after all, banks were too big to fail. In the run-up to the crisis, the investment bank Bear Stearns had been sold off with help from the US government, and the British government had nationalized Northern Rock.

People were still waking up to the fact that this was the most serious crisis to hit the global economy since the Great Depression, while governments did everything they could to maintain stability. Interest rates were cut to an all-time low, austerity measures announced and quantitative easing kicked in. While global economies plunged, large bailout packages were announced; often financed with taxpayers' money.

Back in the 80s and 90s, working in the financial sector was a coveted position. Bankers were respected, even envied, because they did complex 'stuff', lived extremely lavish lives and enjoyed a position of immense power. However, like

Ozymandias,[3] the king of kings, little remains. The mighty fall hard – the financial crisis proved that yet again. *'Look on my works, ye mighty, and despair.'*

Although the world was in a state of utter panic, it didn't seem that there were severe consequences for the big names in the frame; somehow they seemed to get away lightly, and were even rewarded as they left. There were those who were allowed to resign, such as Stan O'Neal, CEO of Merrill Lynch, who collected $161 m in severance pay; in other cases, they were even retained as consultants. When AIG's financial product division lost $11bn, instead of being fired, the CEO, Joseph Cassano, was kept on with the firm at $1m a month to retain his intellectual knowledge.[i]

At the end of the day, the poorest paid the largest price as homes were repossessed, people lost their jobs and unemployment in the US and Europe rose to more than 10%. A report published by Oxford University and the London School of Hygiene and Tropical Medicine states that there were at least an additional 10,000 suicides as a result of the crisis, with rates increasing in the region of 17% from 2007 to 2011.[ii]

The crisis had multiple causes, primarily greed and

---

[3] Poem by Percy Bysshe Shelley

lack of governance. We could blame many parties, including bankers who didn't act in clients' best interests; checkers, such as central banks and regulators, who tolerated it; politicians, who allowed it all to happen by making decisions such as banning the regulation of derivatives (a highly complex financial product); or even the economic backdrop, which may have created a sense of complacency, ultimately leading to a surge in debt since it seemed okay to spend today and pay tomorrow. Warning signs from auditors were ignored as the situation spiraled out of control.

Context is important. How could it be that something that seemed okay in the past seems so unacceptable now, and how was it allowed to continue for so long anyway? Was it willful wrongdoing, negligence, or just excessive complexity introduced by a combination of deregulation, enhanced technology and intricate arrangements that were too difficult for most people to understand?

In a nutshell, the crisis was caused by a combination of failures in financial regulation and corporate governance, firms taking on too much risk, and excessive borrowing by households and Wall Street. It was very hard to pin down accountability, and there were breaches in ethics as we were consumed by greed. Let's take a look at some other key events since then.

Payment Protection Insurance (PPI)

Any mention of the crisis would be incomplete without looking at the scandal associated with Payment Protection Insurance (PPI). This was an insurance product that allowed customers to insure loan repayment if something were to go wrong. Let's assume I took on a mortgage; were I to die, or become ill or disabled, this insurance product would protect my family from the burden of debt. There was nothing wrong with the product in principle; the problem was that it just didn't work. It had some key issues:

- People were led to believe that the insurance was compulsory.
- Sometimes, they were simply unaware that they even had the insurance.
- Sometimes, they already had adequate protection arrangements, so they were paying for extra cover they did not need.
- Many who tried to claim didn't qualify because of hidden or unclear exclusions, such as self-employed people, students or those with existing illnesses.
- Even if people were lucky enough to meet the conditions for a pay-out, it could have been a short-term pay-out that would not fully cover the claim period or the level of

cover would not cover their entire loan – just the interest and not the principal.

In summary, it was well packaged but infused with issues that raised concerns about the intentions, design, eligibility criteria, pricing and sales practices. That is precisely the reason why it is often referred to as a good idea implemented badly.

It was the UK's worst-ever consumer scandal, and two years after it unfolded, firms had already paid in excess of £20bn in fines and compensation to affected customers. Years after the scandal, I was getting calls from companies looking for anyone who might have been mis-sold these insurance vehicles, claiming they could make a claim for compensation on my behalf.

This is only one of the many scandals of this nature that were uncovered after the crisis. However, due to its timing, its widespread impact on society, the size of the bill to put things right (over £20 billion) and resulting media attention, this scandal acted to reinforce the general belief about financial institutions putting their own interest ahead of customers' interest and taking advantage of customers' trust and lack of understanding of complex terms and conditions.

The aftermath

In its wake, the crisis left firms and regulators wondering what needed to be done to ensure that events of this scale never raised their ugly heads again, and so they sought action and evidence to confirm that banks had corrected their behaviour.

The community and customers, quite rightly, felt shaken and let down. In some countries more than others, the image of the industry hit rock bottom and conduct, also referred to as ethics and behaviour, became a topic of heightened attention.

Although many people had not understood all the details of the crisis or been directly impacted, they clearly wanted to see some action that provided assurance and a sense of control, and would convince them that this was water under the bridge. To win back customers' trust, firms focused wholly on reducing examples of bad behaviour – not on increasing examples of good behaviour. Hold on to that thought.

People wanted an assurance that if more issues were to come to light, the tab would be picked up by those who made the mistakes as opposed to innocent taxpayers.

The question then was, how do you get financial

decision-makers to enter the debate, and how do you give a topic as broad and fuzzy as conduct its own serious identity? What would make the financial world sit up and notice that the consequences could be grave?

Beside all the talk about improving business ethics, the sentiment was one of people wanting guarantees that those who breached the rules again would face dire consequences.

The burden of the clean-up fell almost entirely on those working in the financial system as they struggled to convince people that banks had corrected their behaviour. Firms found themselves engulfed in a very stressful environment battling with the mammoth task of remediation and restoration while having lost much of the trust and respect they had been accustomed to.

Sadly, there wasn't a reset button like the one on our broadband routers. It just didn't work like that. We couldn't shut down the banking system, do a cleanup and start over. Correction had to be done in parallel with day-to-day activity. Banks needed to continue to serve customers, gradually switching to new standards of service, and at the same time they had to clean up the sins of the past while maintaining profitability and growth targets in the face of complex technology changes and economic turbulence. Dealing with the added scrutiny such as regulatory visits and heightened media attention was part of the deal.

Comparing this to the London Underground, it would be similar to managing a train crash, while continuing to run all services, repairing the damage and ensuring that regular maintenance and scheduled upgrades were not affected. In our daily lives, I could compare this to hosting guests for an elaborate meal while doing a spring clean and moving home.

For those who thought that bankers had no feelings, the intensity and range of emotions witnessed here could put a Bollywood drama to shame.

You sense frustration – with the industry being left to deal with the cleanup and the burden of image restoration, while key culprits had cashed out and were enjoying retirement on luxurious golf courses. As one person said to me, 'I feel like I am being punished for the mistakes that the naughty children had made.'

You sense chaos – primarily because of the lack of any precedent. Boards would have liked to cut a cheque to clean up behaviour, but how do you resolve something that stems from the boardroom? With chaos comes disappointment caused by failed attempts and constantly moving goalposts.

You sense opportunity – in service providers who are able to link their business propositions to conduct, creating solutions to help organisations as they deal with the enormous task of correcting their behaviour. The solutions range from training courses that teach good judgement to technology solutions such as databases that are capable of maintaining audit trails of customer interactions, so that banks can prove their innocence.

You sense cynicism – from purists in risk management who, having managed risk for years, believe that the entire commotion is just a short-lived, attention-seeking gimmick. Some people dealing with customers feel that nothing has really changed, and they make it their mantra to go with the flow and do as told until the regulators declare them clean again.

You sense fear – because there are people who just aren't sure of themselves any more. They simply don't understand what they did wrong and what they need to do differently. These people feel overwhelmed and for them, there is so much going on that they struggle to take a stance without worrying that their decisions could come back to bite them. I often find that this set of people have simply stopped taking any personal risk as they ensure that everything they do is fully approved by someone else – a boss, a committee, anyone but them. It would, in their view, be risky, almost stupid, to make decisions when the rules of the game were constantly changing and red cards dished out in plenty.

So what needs to change? First, let's take a look at what is happening around us.

'Unfortunately the people who did best in good times were those who took the most risk and nobody questioned them. The bottom line is that in the good times, nobody asks the right questions and in the bad times you are not going to get the right answers.'

Lex van Dam

2. Is bad behaviour limited to banks?

Our conduct is what we do when nobody is watching and we believe that no one will ever find out. So we have to ask, how would we conduct ourselves if there were no controls and no checks? Would it not be natural to want to do the right thing by our country, our family, our customers and all those who place their trust in us?

Many of the news stories I see have a conduct element in them. It's odd because as we get savvier with time, I would expect to see fewer issues. Perhaps the increase is better explained by reduced tolerance and an active media as opposed to degradation in our ethical fabric. Also, as we are exposed to more stories of poor behaviours, maybe we develop a subconscious need to distance ourselves, justifying in our own minds that we are not one of those people.

I wonder if we are just splitting into types – those of us that cause issues and those who take it upon ourselves to uphold moral values, making it our role to bring events to light calling out unacceptable behaviour. Or are we the same person?

Over the last few years, I have been noticing conduct issues in various fields involving everyone from doctors to priests, parents to teachers and bankers to politicians. In July 2015, the Commons speaker, John Bercow, made headlines when details of his travel and accommodation costs were revealed by use of the Freedom of Information (FoI) Act. His expenses, branded obscene, include a £172 bill for being driven 0.7 miles from parliament to Carlton House Terrace in London. He also clocked a £367 bill to take a car to Luton (30-odd miles) to deliver a speech on the expenses scandal and MPs' efforts to restore their reputation. Pot, kettle, black.

'Life is short. Have an affair,' is the slogan of Ashley Madison, the online dating site for married people. In July 2015, the site was hacked by a group called Impact Team, raising issues of morals in society and a general feeling of disgust as to why people would use such a site. Yet between them, sites such as Ashley Madison and Illicit Encounters have millions of users – and the users are none other than the likes of you and me.

Before we try to resolve the issue of bad behaviour, let's remember not to single out the banking industry. Banks are only a microcosm of the society we live in, and behaviours demonstrated at these firms are no different to those displayed in Parliament, in relationships or in sport – albeit to a greater or lesser degrees. Not all bankers are criminals and not all priests are pure.

My effort to establish that the conduct issue transcends banks is not one of justification by citing its pervasiveness but an appeal to stop the isolation of this, or any other industry for that matter. This recognition, however, does not alleviate the need to fix things.

I am a middle-class mum and my children sometimes insist on having things that other children have, e.g. more pocket money or unlimited internet access. I always say to them that they are my primary concern and it is not for me to make decisions for other children. What you will not find me saying is that I made decisions for my children based on what everyone else was doing. Just as parents decide what is right for their children given their unique circumstances, your business is your child and it is incumbent upon you to decide what is and isn't right. There is no getting away from accountability, but the good news is that when we care enough, we will want to be accountable.

3. What customers really want?

Chicken and chips vs. horsemeat scandals

A little while ago, I was walking home with my daughter and she stopped to buy chicken and chips. She needed £1.

I gave her the money.

She walked beside me, tucking into her meal. It didn't look too bad, and I asked for a bite.

Reluctantly, she obliged.

I bit into it to find a bone. I reacted, 'Ewwww, it has bones!'

She replied, 'We just got something for £1 from a corner shop. What were you expecting, KFC chicken popcorn?'

She hit my conduct nerve. That, for me, is right at the heart of conduct.

Giving customers what they expect. The right product, to the right customer, at a fair price. No hidden messages.

Who was the customer?

My daughter.

Did she understand fully what she was going to buy?

Yes.

Did she get what she was expecting to get?

Yes.

Did I like the product?

Not really — but that doesn't matter; I'm not the customer.

Let's map her journey as a customer.

She saw a board by a shop that told her what's on offer.

There weren't any warning signs, no age restrictions, allergy warnings etc.

The price was clear and it seemed all right.

She decided she wanted chicken and chips, went in and got some.

She got the order in decent time and liked what she got.

Simple.

She didn't fall ill after she ate it.

All good.

Now let's compare that with the horsemeat scandal.

The scandal started in 2013 in the UK, when people realised that some of the products they had bought, thinking them to be 100% processed beef, actually contained horsemeat.

People were outraged. As the story evolved, it became clear that a number of UK supermarket chains were affected. There were multiple product recalls and it put a spotlight on the entire supply chain.

Was it about horsemeat *per se*?

I don't think so. You could argue that if horsemeat was served as a delicacy, or promoted by famous chefs, people might have paid a higher price to get it.

Horsemeat is a safe product so it's not a safety issue. It is certainly not about the meat.

The issue here is one of losing faith, to a point where you ask yourself what you can actually believe and who can you trust? A feeling of being let down – not by one person on one occasion, but by multiple people, in a systematic manner, over a period of time.

It's a story that goes right to the heart of breaching customers' trust.

Did the product contain what it says on the tin?

No.

Did people feel that they have been lied to?

Yes.

Was there any physical harm?

No, but that's not the point.

Did customers lost out financially?

It could be argued that they did, since they didn't get what they paid for. Customers wanted a meal and they got a meal, but the meal wasn't what they believed it to be.

When industries conduct themselves in this way, poor reputation follows. While the backdrop of my book is primarily financial, the principles that I explore are generic, transcending industries, countries, organisations and genders; they stand the test of time, because the issue of conduct is not limited to the UK or to banks.

Customers across the globe seek more transparency and accountability. As the world gets flatter[4] and organisations become more complex, it is becoming more difficult than ever to pin down accountability. Does accountability need to be pinned down, or does the very principle need to be refreshed so that it lends itself to the dynamics of today's fast-paced, complex and wired world?

Let's take a look at some of the regulatory responses to this need for change.

---

[4] Thomas L. Friedman's *The World is Flat* refers to the globalised world of the twenty-first century.

4. Changing regulatory expectations

As the need for a culture change became obvious, regulators worldwide began to take note of the need for better conduct, also widely referred to as ethical behaviour or conduct risk; i.e. the risk of making poor decisions that serve firms' interests over clients' interests.

The UK regulator, set up the Financial Services Act of 2012, created a new system for regulating financial services to protect and improve the UK's economy with the purpose of ensuring that markets work well so that customers get a fair deal.[iii] Its objectives were to:

- Maintain and ensure the integrity of the market
- Regulate financial services firms so that they give consumers a fair deal
- Ensure the financial services market is competitive

The newly formed Financial Conduct Authority (FCA) was responsible for conduct supervision, and its powers included the ability to ban products that posed unacceptable risk to customers, and even ban products for up to 12 months without consultation.[iv] The aim was to ensure that only the right firms, run by the right people, selling the right products to the right consumers, were approved to do business.

The FCA in the UK has referred to conduct risk in the context of 'consumer detriment arising from the wrong products ending up in the wrong hands, and the detriment to society of people not being able to get access to the right products'. The key being that customers get financial services and products that meet their needs from firms they trust; markets are stable, sound, resilient with transparent information, pricing and otherwise; organisations are outcome-based rather than process-based, and there is early intervention before client detriment occurs.

Other regulators placed a similar focus on ethics. The US Financial Industry Regulatory Authority (FINRA) states, 'independent regulation plays a critical role in America's financial system – by enforcing high ethical standards, bringing the necessary resources and expertise to regulation and enhancing investor safeguards and market integrity – all at no cost to taxpayers.'

It also states that 'every investor in America relies on one thing: fair financial markets. That's why FINRA works every day to ensure that:

- every investor receives the basic protections they deserve;

- anyone who sells a securities product has been tested, qualified and licensed;
- every securities product advertisement used is truthful, and not misleading;
- any securities product sold to an investor is suitable for that investor's needs; and
- investors receive complete disclosure about the investment product before purchase.'

Let's take a look at some regulatory fines since the crisis. In the UK, the FCA handed out its highest number of fines in eight years in 2013. There were 48 fines, adding up to a total of around £475 million. In 2012, there were 53 fines, adding up to £372 million. Compare this with 2006, when there were 52 fines, adding up to £23 million.

In terms of how these amounts impact the banks, according to a BBC report,[v] between 2011 and 2014, Britain's largest banks paid 60% of their profits in fines and repayments to customers. The accountants analysed the results of Royal Bank of Scotland, Lloyds, HSBC, Barclays and Standard Chartered. The total in penalties for the four years from 2011 to 2014 was £38.7bn.

Fines in 2013 related mainly to Libor[5] manipulation,

---

[5] London inter-bank lending rate. This is the interest rate that banks charge each other for loans, and is considered to be one of the most important interest rates in finance. It helps to

mis-selling and control failings. HSBC, Royal Bank of Scotland, Swiss bank UBS and US banks JP Morgan Chase, Citibank and Bank of America were fined a collective £2.6bn by UK and US regulators for their attempts to manipulate foreign exchange rates.

As an employee on the other side, I feel a touch of embarrassment each time the industry is shamed again. I like to believe that I do a decent job, but something just doesn't add up. The fines are huge and have lasting effects on balance sheets and morale. Rushing through our days as headlines fades one into another, we may not register minute details, yet the constant feed leaves lasting impressions – somewhat like new singles that appear on iTunes. We love a tune for a while, gradually moving on to the next chart topper, and over time we develop a sense of what's on trend.

I wonder, despite all the fines and clean-up activity, whether customers genuinely see a change for the better. Do they feel more secure? Do they feel that they can now trust the banking sector more? How frequently is prioritisation of issues based on customers telling us that something is hurting them? Like banks, do they feel more burdened?

---

decide the price of transactions and is used as a measure of trust in the financial system because it is indicative of the financial health of banks.

Sometimes I ask myself if I felt the pain of the financial crisis. What specifically hurt me? Does it not hurt anymore? Has it become easier or more difficult? And, if we were to do a regression analysis[6] of the key changes that have in fact improved customers' lives, how much of the improvement can be attributed to a conscious focus on culture and conduct? Perhaps, as a customer, I am now more secure, and I just don't realise it.

Several years later, customers still received calls from the refund industry set up around the errors associated with the PPI product. Some of the related refund adverts didn't shy away from using the names of the large banks, creating a perception that they may be sites set up by the banks themselves. I wonder what customers experience when they enter into a transaction believing this to be the bank itself, only to realise later that they were dealing with someone else. Could they, perhaps, feel that they have gone from being victims of one mis-selling scandal to another?

The key question around the fines themselves is whether banks will ease into this regime as the new norm, making it a habit to set aside some capital to meet these expenses, as we do for a rainy day; or will

---

[6] A statistical tool used to investigate relationships between variables to ascertain how one variable affects another.

they correct their behaviour so as to alleviate the need for such fines? Will regulators reduce the penalties or will firms be driven out of business, potentially resorting to other countries and losing key figureheads to other industries? Will there be a time where bankers simply stop taking risks as firms learn to cope with this phase of isolation, shame, fear, fatigue and lack of motivation? Only time can tell. I am not questioning that we need to correct the system – most definitely we should. My concern here is how we should go about it.

Getting it right …

A need for change that no one denies,

Openness and action, no room for lies.

We all want to move, not just sit and stare…

But how exactly should we get there?

Just how much regulation is enough?

It seems to be getting a little tough.

Tough may be right, or it may have a fall-out,

Do I have all the answers? I very much doubt …

Pick up the papers from the stands.

Oh the terrible bad banks!

They're at it again,

Horrible bad men...

They've got to get in line,

Or pay a hefty fine.

With all change, there is the doer and the done,

While views may differ, the purpose should be one.

Of course we need to get it right; it's not a matter so light.

For our economy and this world, we want futures to be bright.

As I spend time in this space...

And make my way through this maze...

There are thoughts and reflections

And some interesting conversations.

Chipping at it, bit by bit,

This book is my story of how I see it.

Through classic mistakes and lessons to be learnt,

On why we wait until our fingers are burnt?

Whether we manage change, or lead teams,

We sometimes miss the basics, or so it seems.

But it's not all doom and gloom,

Some great examples loom.

As the story gets told...

As connections unfold...

Read, think, and take a moment to blink,

Somewhere in there, you will find the sync.

5. Today's scenario

Before we get into solutions, let's take a moment to appreciate day-to-day life in this sector and understand some of the concerns and challenges that the industry faces today. This background needs to be understood because future solutions must be designed bearing this landscape in mind.

Increasingly complex business structures

Organisational hierarchies are now more complex, with matrix-like management structures where departments are stacked like rows and columns (also called horizontals and verticals) in a way that no one person can be fully responsible for the end-to-end product or service. How this may pan out in reality might be somewhat like walking into a restaurant for a meal where no one takes ownership of your entire experience – while managers may run the restaurant and manage its people, some aspects such as the lighting or the cleaning may not be part of what they control or care for. Parts of a business may be handed-off to external providers and even sub-providers, making it very difficult to understand exactly how all the pieces fit together. In addition, businesses may operate in global jurisdictions, which means that they must satisfy an increasingly diverse customer base and meet varied regulatory requirements. The increasing complexity often combined with rapid growth and digitisation can make it difficult to determine accountability – a bit like the horsemeat scandal. The resulting scenario has a bearing on day-to-day affairs, causing gaps and overlaps in work, slowing down decisions and making it difficult to determine who is in charge of overseeing what. Most importantly, it becomes a major obstacle when something goes wrong and someone needs to own up, take responsibility and put things right.

To draw a parallel with driving a complex machine, it may be that one person watches the brakes while another manages the accelerator; overall, however, someone has to know when the car is going off the road, and passengers need to know who they can rely upon to get it back on track. It is equally crucial for those in the driver's seat to recognise that they are in fact the people that everyone is relying on.

While it seems impossible to do away with these overly complex structures, at least in the short run, they need to be simplified or at least well understood.

Complex supply chains

In the horsemeat scandal, according to the BBC, investigations found that horsemeat sold as beef originated from Romanian slaughterhouses and was then sold to a Dutch food trader, then on to a Cypriot trader and on again to a French firm.[vi]

When a product travels from Romania to the Netherlands, and on to Greece and France before it makes its way to a UK supermarket and eventually our homes, it can get very tricky and expensive to establish who failed the system. It doesn't take much to bring the chain down. When any link of such an enormous chain feels pressure of any sort, the entire chain is put to the test. Convergence of poor controls with poor intention or even just lack of attention spells disaster.

When any part of this chain succumbs to greed to the point where their desire for profits becomes greater than their desire to do the right thing, the controls will have to kick in. This could be compared to safety measures at home. We advise children to keep away from sockets, and trust that they will all understand and follow the guidance, but then just to be sure, we cover the socket too. Controls are those socket covers.

Applying today's standards to yesterday's behaviour

Due to regulatory evolution and changing standards, firms are finding out the hard way that what was acceptable yesterday is simply not good enough today. Hence they are waking up to find large numbers of clients who haven't been served correctly in the past and need to be put right. They may have been served correctly by the standards that were in place then but not according to the standards that are in place now.

If you translate this to the automobile industry, it may be similar to multiple product recalls to ensure that vehicles made yesterday meet the safety standards of today. This would mean not just rectifying products and services of the past to meet the standards of today, but also ensuring that the standards being set today will be able to stand the test of time.

I must add here that I don't refer to Volkswagen's issues relating to cheating on emission tests that surfaced in September 2015, although of course there too employees were left to wonder what this meant for them.

Keeping up with the fourth generation

Technology has been moving so rapidly for such a long time that it's almost always one of the key things to bear in mind when determining any organisation's landscape. The statistics in this area are nothing short of mindboggling. Some suggest that 90% of the world's data was generated in the last two years (2014), and other suggest that data will continue to double itself every one and a half years.

Like everything else, conduct is not untouched by the changes in technology. JP Morgan's UK wealth management business was fined £3.1 million for failing to keep complete and up-to-date information on client objectives, risk profile and risk appetite, placing clients at risk of receiving inappropriate investment advice. The regulator's argument was that the firm's computer systems did not allow sufficient client information to be retained. The issue was one of the system or technology, as opposed to human failure or a failure of controls. While this is a conduct issue in the broadest sense (because it puts customers at risk of poor advice), root causes include factors such as process design and technology capability.

Banks are therefore finding their ground amidst disruptive technologies[7] and exploring options that can increase efficiency while giving customers more choice in how they wish to bank. For example, a traditional wealth business that normally relied heavily on deep relationships between clients and their bankers may look for ways to use technology

---

[7] A disruptive technology is one that disrupts or displaces an existing technology and forces firms to think differently, e.g. smart phones disrupting personal computers or Wikipedia disrupting traditional encyclopaedias.

such as mobile banking or robot advisors[8] to see how best it can leverage technology to offer more choice to existing customers who will want information to be more readily available, stay relevant for Gen X and Gen Y investors, or even to reach out to others who may be unable to afford traditional wealth management as the technology may help reduce the overall cost of service. As customers get used to click-and-collect type multichannel services, traditional firms often fear being overtaken by more agile, technology-savvy organisations such as Alibaba, Google or Amazon. With the European Union recognising Bitcoins as a currency, technology is set to cause disruption in more ways than we may have imagined.

When addressing behaviours, we need to be fully cognisant of such external pressures and other similar internal pressures that may be unique to an organisation. Any correction should seek to use this information to its advantage as opposed to viewing it as an obstacle. Organisations need to explore questions such as how best to leverage technology to support firms with their story of change. Alternatively, they may choose to continue dealing

---

[8] Robo-advisers are online wealth management services that provide automated, algorithm-based advice based on questions used to understand details such as our attitude towards risk, our level of sophistication and our personal objectives. This may be with or without human intervention.

with scenarios in isolation, treating conduct as an unrelated temporary debate, one to be paid lip service until the storm calms down. Organisations often wonder if conduct correction and conduct checks should be bolted on to every process, every job, and every committee in the hope that someday it would be norm for every decision to have undergone severe conduct scrutiny, in which case we will be living the absolute utopia. Or should they be integrated into the system as we design the future?

Now that we have a common understanding of the backdrop, let's look into this fuzzy world of conduct because before we solve a problem, we need to understand what it means.

6. Getting to grips with conduct

What's in the barn?

One day when my son was seven, he brought home a book. I believe it was called *What's Behind the Barn?* In the story, there was an animal behind the barn, and a few animals gathered outside were trying to make sense of what was inside. The door to the barn was shut, and one by one the animals came to the door, took a peek and went away describing what they saw. For example, the cat said, 'I see big brown eyes'; and the snake said, 'I see a hairy tail.' Based on the various descriptions, they imagined that there was a huge monstrous animal inside; only to find that it was just a tiny little rabbit.

The conduct experience seems similar. With everyone having taken a peek; we have imagined a large beast, somehow finding ourselves scampering about to remedy things based on what each has seen. Everyone has an understanding of conduct because the word itself is not new to any of us, but we have a long way to go if we want to get consistent in our understanding and approach – and get it right.

For example, some firms have established conduct as a type of risk, in the sense that they see poor conduct as a risk that they may harm customers, and that must therefore be constantly managed. Others have taken a more values-based approach in that good conduct is something they aspire to and consider especially when making strategic decisions. In day-to-day application, some choose to focus attention on areas that could give rise to poor conduct or have done so in the past, such as poorly designed products and incorrect distribution (such as PPI), unclear communication, performance incentives that may entice employees into making unsuitable sales, and so on, while others seek to ensure that they can demonstrate how they have given due attention to conduct when managing the business. There may be others simply watching regulatory guidance and adapting accordingly.

Perhaps with conduct being nebulous and in its infancy, such variation is to be expected while it matures in definition, understanding and implementation. After all, each business needs to define what is right for it; no one size fits all. The only thing we need to realise is that such trial and error often comes at a cost; financial and non-financial. In the case of conduct, financial costs could include the costs of managing large change programmes which may include costs such as training and project management, while non-financial costs could include employee uncertainty, incomparable industry-level data, increased anxiety due to changing goalposts etc., which we will touch upon in the chapter relating to high stakes.

Coming back to our story, when this animal is out of the barn, we may realise that a lot of what we built based on our limited understanding (although with good intentions) wasn't really required. For example, I thought this was going to be a dog so I built a kennel, but that wasn't required since this fuzzy thing is only a rabbit after all.

The points of confusion

Most businesses are in a rush to improve their behaviour – or sometimes, to create the impression that they have done so. Boards want to know where the culture stands today, where it needs to be, by when it will be done and how much it will cost. On the other hand, managers who handle business at a day-to-day level ask different questions:

- How is conduct different to meeting legal requirements?
- What are the key conduct risks for organisations today?
- What are the top conduct risks on the horizon?
- How do you define horizon? Where does it start and where does it end? Is it 0-18 months, or somewhere else in the future?
- How much time should I spend worrying about risks in the future that may never actually crystallise as opposed to events of

the past that I need to clean up? This causes a strain on my capacity to deal with issues of today, so am I not creating more issues for tomorrow again?

- How do you define the scope? If this building were to collapse, and we were unable to serve customers, would that be a conduct risk?
- If the bank next door is fined for improper conduct, is it incumbent upon me to check that the same issues don't exist in my firm?
- Should conduct not be something for Human Resources to manage; after all they deal with the soft side of things – the people aspect?
- Should we have conduct champions to fly the conduct flag and keep us right?
- Could it be that the creation of champions would make the rest feel that upholding conduct was someone else's job?
- How is conduct risk different to operational risk?
- Is it not just operational risk gone horribly wrong?
- There is no such thing as conduct risk, it doesn't exist. When will you stop pretending that It does?
- What specifically do I need to do differently?
- How do you demonstrate that you practise good conduct – by speaking about conduct or speaking about more customers?

- Why does it sometimes feel like a box-ticking exercise?

Questions are a great way to get the pulse of the industry. Before organisations jump into solutions, they must articulate what conduct means to them and their firm.

Defining what 'is' and 'is not' conduct

Nobody quite agrees on what conduct risk means or where its boundaries are set. It is often a case of implementing change based on a broad, all-encompassing definition without a start and stop point, and one that can cover almost every risk and every event in an organisation.

This may be because different regulators have included conduct in their taxonomy in different ways as their own understanding continues to evolve. As businesses transcend geographic boundaries more than ever before, this poses a challenge for local branches of global firms who continually absorb these changing views from head office and local regulators. For example, in the UK, the concept of Treating Customer Fairly (TCF) has, in a way, been subsumed by conduct that is an improvement over TCF. The conduct thinking retains the TCF ethic while extending further to bring in aspects such as doing what is right for the market (touching upon topics such as anti-money-laundering initiatives) and is more proactive with a lot of focus on accountability. I believe however, that TCF reporting continues to be a regulatory requirement in Africa.

This may mean not just discovering that the animal in the barn is different from what we first imagined it to be, but that there are more barns and more pets around the farm.

One good way to resolve this may be to build something adaptable that could meet varied requirements. The good news is that it's basic stuff – and the bad news is that it's basic stuff. Common sense is not common behaviour and basics need to be explained.

Establishing clear principles

I believe that in its purest form, conduct is how you conduct yourself; especially bearing in mind the responsibility you carry. It is the moral compass of an organisation.

Managing conduct then requires a set of principles that form part of a tool kit and are to be used in spirit to guide decisions, not as an exhaustive checklist requiring attestation at each decision point. The concept is similar to how managers and leaders use principles of management such as those published by Henri Fayol in 1916. We often use the principles such authority and responsibility and division of work without referring to them as the 14 principles. A hundred years on, as we subconsciously apply these principles to inform decisions, rather than as a checklist to validate managerial decisions, they simply become a part of how we do things.

As parents, we have a set of principles that we use to set a good example for children. Based on our upbringing and beliefs, we create our views of what is okay and what is not okay – usually leading by example. We then use this belief to determine the most appropriate behaviour in a given situation. Even as children we learn to conduct ourselves in a certain way when with parents. While there are books on good parenting, and some specific dos and don'ts, box ticking of any sort, in my view, would damage the authenticity and spontaneity of the relationship. In most cases, good conduct comes naturally, because we care. In some cases, we know there are certain things we need to watch out for. Sometimes, we slip and then we look for ways to correct ourselves. That too is perfectly okay.

Recognising the pervasive nature of conduct

The responsibility of making good conduct decisions is not limited to one person or one committee. It is upon everyone in an organisation to accept and acknowledge that their decisions and actions could impact end outcomes. However, the nature of the impact may vary, e.g. bankers who deal with clients could have a more direct and immediate effect while the contribution of support teams who may be designing systems for tomorrow may not be visible until the system is actually live and in use. I'm often asked questions such as what conduct has to do with technology, or Human Resources – a lot. Just as it is important for everyone to recognise that they play a role, it is equally important to recognise that it is something that we do day-in, day-out as opposed to something that needs to be done at specific meetings and specific times – less like counting five a day[9] and more like living a healthy life in totality.

Accepting that people change their mind

In the comedy *Daddy Day Care*, Eddie Murphy plays Charlie, who works in product development at a large food company when he and a colleague suddenly lose their jobs and are forced to become stay-at-home fathers. During this time, Charlie sees a gap in the market for good childcare and the two fathers set up their own child-care facility, Daddy Day Care.

---

[9] Refers to national campaigns that encourage people to eat five portions of fruit and vegetable a day based on recommendations by the World Health Organisation.

After spending time with children at the day care, including his own son Ben, Charlie returns to work for a short time and is asked to create an advert for Cotton Candy Puffs. In an effort to inspire the advert, Charlie is asked for the first word that came to mind when he heard of Cotton Candy Puffs. While the others are thinking of the business opportunity on offer, Charlie looks at a drawing Ben had given to him. The picture is titled *Ben and Daddy*. Charlie looks up, and to everyone's astonishment, says 'cavities'. This isn't the same Charlie who left the firm; something has changed. Time spent with Ben and other children has changed his paradigm, instilling a sense of responsibility so that he no longer feels good putting a whole-hearted effort into supporting something that isn't necessarily ideal for these kids.

For those asking what conduct has to do with legal requirements, this is that difference. It is perfectly legal to advertise Cotton Candy Puffs. I accept that my children eat them sometimes, but for Charlie, it wasn't something he wanted to do any more.

What is more interesting is that it seemed appropriate to the others and even to Charlie before he established Daddy Day Care, but he changed his mind. He wasn't going to stop anyone else doing it, but he wasn't going to do it.

That really fine line is conduct. When something is legal and everyone else might be doing it, but an inner voice tells you, 'C'mon you've got to stand up for what you believe in' – that voice is conduct. You can all it your conscience or, as Jack Welch would put it, your gut.

While the phrase 'doing the right thing' is bandied about in the conduct context, at the heart of it is the recognition that the right thing for me may not be the right thing for you, and what seems right to me today may not seem so to me tomorrow.

We are humans and not machines. The planet evolves and we do too. It is okay to evolve, okay to change your mind and okay to be different. You just need to be able to explain your decisions. When you make a mistake, you need to be able to put your hands up and say sorry, and be ready to fix the mess.

Accepting that right and wrong can vary by culture

In Tamal Bandyopadhyay's book *A Bank for the Buck*, the author narrates the history of India's HDFC bank. Tamal cites a conversation between two individuals involved in the bank's creation, Deepak and Aditya, where Deepak was trying to convince Aditya to join the inaugural team. He said that Aditya was based in Singapore and would need to move to India with his wife and 10-year-old daughter. The author writes,

'Deepak told Aditya he was on the Board of trustees of the famed Bombay Scottish School in Mumbai, and getting admission for Amrita (Aditya's Daughter) would be a cake walk.'

Being of Indian origin and having studied there, I know just how prevalent and acceptable this is. It is common practice for people to use their power, position, money or any connection whatsoever to secure preferential treatment, particularly when it comes to matters such as schooling. These favours, as they are normally called, could range from skipping queues for a hairdresser's appointment to landing jobs for relatives. Becoming the unwritten rules of society, they morph into mini status symbols.

From a conduct standpoint, if my daughter had been denied admission to the same school because I did not know anyone on the board of trustees, this incident would infuriate me.

Yet, in the fight between the haves and have-nots, and the day-to-day struggle to make ends meet, conduct is not the first thing that comes to mind — finding a connection is.

Understanding that poor conduct is not limited to culpable harm

Sometimes people may be impacted poorly by our

actions even though it wasn't our intention to do so. Damaging consequences could very easily be a by-product of our pursuit of something. In the example of the school admission, we need to bear in mind that India is a country with a population of more than 1.2 billion people where good schooling is a finite resource and parents are in a rush to secure the best for their children. People's efforts to beat the system emanate from desperation to provide for their families as best they can, not from any active desire to wrong anyone.

That's the exciting journey of conduct. Conduct is not binary, it never has been and it never will be. While bystanders may judge decisions from a narrower standpoint, for those making the call, it could be that everything from their past and present is screaming out for priority, with multiple variables at odds with one another so that conduct becomes a balancing act; a dilemma as opposed to an obvious answer to a logical process. When people are exposed for poor decisions, in addition to focusing on the fact that they didn't mean to cause harm, they should be able to paint the fuller picture and explain what else was on their mind.

Accepting that even well-meaning actions can have poor consequences

Sometimes, even well-meaning actions can have

unintended consequences. Let's take the issue of begging. Generally speaking, we all mean well when we give some money to a beggar.

Let's look at it in a slightly different way. Begging is an organised crime in India, often run by underworld gangs in a very systematic manner. The twitter account @storypicker shared a short powerful video in an attempt to raise awareness of how Indians may be contributing to this crime by funding criminal gangs while believing that they are only helping the poor.

In the short video uploaded by Indi Viral, a student in Delhi conducted a social experiment and went to beg on the streets. The video showed the student getting into the mindset and attire of a beggar before hitting the road to test how much he might be able to earn. Collecting Rs. 200 in just two hours, he believed that this would total Rs. 30,000 a month. In comparison, call-centre employees make about Rs. 25,000 a month.

The message that the students were trying to communicate was that through our random acts of kindness we were all making significant contributions to organised crime gangs.

There are other similar stories. In the UK, the chancellor announced a 38% rise in the minimum wage over five years from 2015, also called the new living wage. While being a generally welcome move, it is not without poor consequences for some sectors: labour-intensive organisations in particular will be impacted by the combination of this change and a new auto-enrolment pension scheme. Some establishments may be unable to bear the added cost or pass it on to customers, and may thus be forced to close down. Therefore, good intentions may drive poor outcomes and it may not be possible to do what is right by everyone all the time.

Accepting that many of us cheat, just a little bit

In his book *The Honest Truth about Dishonesty*, Dan Ariely explores the causes of dishonesty, highlighting that cheating in day-to-day life is not necessarily due to one guy doing a cost-benefit analysis and stealing lots of money. If it were so, we would be cheating each time we got a chance. It is more often than not an outcome of many people who quietly justify taking a little bit of cash or a little bit of merchandise over and over again. Ariely looks into what causes dishonest behaviour, concluding that on the one hand, we want to benefit from the cheating to satisfy a rational economic motivation, while on the other hand, we want to be able to view ourselves as wonderful human beings to satisfy our psychological motivation to be good people.

He explains that it is through our capacity for flexible reasoning and rationalisation that we reap the benefits of dishonesty while maintaining a positive image of ourselves. In doing so, we often cheat only to the point where we can benefit from cheating while still being able to maintain a positive view of ourselves. This explains why many people cheat a little bit (like picking up a pen or notepad) and very few people cheat a lot (like picking up cupboards full of stationery). This seems an accurate reflection of society as we see it – fewer bank robberies and more shoplifters. You only need to look around to see how real this is.

The banking crisis appears to be a combination of a few big events that can be apportioned to genuinely wilful criminal acts and – far more often – to oversight, shoddy processes, poorly defined accountability and poor controls, or minor incidents of 'cheating' where the bankers, just like the rest of us, didn't think too much of their actions' potential because everyone was doing it. The next point looks into the impact of what everyone else is doing.

Understanding that culture drives behaviour

Let's take a look at our tendencies to 'go with the culture'. In the film *Unfriended*, a group of teenagers were trapped in an online chat with an unseen figure, billie227, who sought vengeance for a shaming video that had led Laura to kill herself a year earlier. At first the friends thought that this was someone hacking into Laura's account, but it soon became clear that this person wanted revenge. They eventually realise that it was Laura using the id billie227, and that it was the anniversary of her death.

The anonymous billie227 asked questions on Laura's behalf, such as who posted the video and why.

Laura texted Blaire: Why did you do this? [Send]

Blaire texted back: I thought it was okay to do, coz everyone was doing it. [Send]

'I didn't mean any harm, I promise.'

Delete, 'I promise'.

'I am sorry.' [Send]

By the end of the film, all the friends are killed by what is believed to be Laura's ghost. I wonder if the group of friends may have acted differently if they had understood the extent of the trauma that the incident would inflict on Laura, enough for it to have driven her to commit suicide. It's classic error of judgement, and may be an outcome of the social pressure teenagers face to conform to a certain cool factor just to fit in and belong. Also, as an increasing amount of interactions happen online, the remoteness makes it somewhat easier to distance ourselves from the consequences of our actions.

This reminds me of an incident where my daughter told me that she was having an argument with someone on Instagram and, in the midst of the argument, the other girl deleted her Instagram account. I could see that my daughter felt bad because the girl who had deleted her account had more than 5,000 followers which, in Instagram speak, meant that she was fairly popular, and recreating that level of followership might take a while. We had a chat and then my daughter found the girl on Twitter and apologised to her. Children need to be taught. Adults too.

A film such as *Unfriended* shows the unintended consequences your action could have. What worries me is that in our drive to address urgent issues, we allow important issues to linger and escalate before attempting to fix them. At some level, we may actually be driving these behaviours by rewarding people who resolve crises while those who work to sustain performance levels barely get acknowledged.

While the financial world cleans up its act through increased regulation, redress and fines, the online world seems to be facing similar challenges. Underneath all of this, we are all trying to resolve conduct practices in society. There is a place for fines and punishments, but more importantly, there is a need for more proactive action and warning; action that keeps us in control as opposed to action that forces us to regain control.

In a scenario bearing some similarity to the film, Tom Hayes,[vii] when questioned about his role in rigging Libor rates, told the jury that he was simply participating in a widespread and generally accepted practice and that he never thought what he was doing was wrong. The first person to be found guilty by British jury of rigging Libor rates, he was given a 14-year prison sentence, the judge saying that it was important to send a powerful deterrent message to the rest of the banking industry.

Knowing your facts

Whatever my view on conduct and its dilemmas, it is important to get the facts right. In the UK, the FCA has introduced the Senior Managers Regime (IAR) that is expected to effect on 7 March 2016. Key points related to the implementation of this regime include that immediate focus will be on a set of senior decision managers; other finer details include a reverse burden of proof whereby individuals could be presumed culpable in the event of regulatory requirements being breached when they were responsible unless they can demonstrate otherwise.[10] There will also be the introduction of a new criminal offence in relation to senior managers taking a decision which causes a relevant firm to fail; this will be punishable by up to seven years in prison and/or an unlimited fine.

At the very least, keeping on the right side of conduct will become a little more complex. It will be interesting to see how the regime unfolds as decisions go on trial and await verdicts more binary in nature. This may be simpler in cases of wilful harm, but for the decisions that consider global parameters, have global consequences both immediate and long-term, and tread fine lines between judgement and fact, it will be interesting to see how we separate the right from the wrong, and who gets to decide. But for that, we will need to wait until 2016. The run-up to March 2016 will be interesting too. With industry recruitment forecasts suggesting that implementation of the regime was one of the key focus areas for organisations, and recruiters seeking change experts to support implementation, it may be right to believe that no efforts will be spared in landing this right. Perhaps key people may consider alternative careers or insurance covers such as malpractice insurance (also called personal liability insurance).

---

[10] As I progress to publish, the reverse burden of proof is expected to be replaced by a duty of responsibility.

This is common in the medical profession as doctors and other professionals cover themselves for damage or injury caused by negligence on their part. In the medical profession, this is one of the most expensive types of insurance, and premiums vary depending upon the type of medicine, local laws, etc. Parallel variables in financial services could be the nature of the firm, size of business and past fines in related businesses. If current fines are anything to go by, premiums could be significant. I wonder if the costs will find their way back to customers who we want to protect in the first place.

'Unfortunately, accountability is one of those concepts that everyone is in the favour of, but nobody knows how to make work – like synergy, or maxi dresses.'

John Oliver

'When written in Chinese, the word "crisis" is composed of two characters. One represents danger and the other represents opportunity.'

John F. Kennedy

7. Why the stakes are high

The stakes are high at both ends – while it is too risky to ignore conduct-related changes, landing them wrong could be risky too. Difficult as it is to get to grips with, we owe it to our business to get this right.

It's expensive – whichever way you look at it

Burning 60% of profits in fines and redress is not something firms can take lightly or allow to continue. The impact of this may be that firms get drawn to the other end of the spectrum, finding themselves guilty of hasty implementation as they rush to convert every hint of regulatory guidance into deployable actions.

As an example, over 2014 there was significant regulatory attention on senior management, and words such as 'tone from the top' were commonly used. Firms' agendas therefore, were heavily focused on getting their senior leaders over the line with respect to their understanding of conduct. Then in May 2015, comments made by Martin Wheatley, then CEO of the FCA, suggested that banks' middle management was a regulatory blind spot in the effort to restore trust in financial services and that its importance was being underplayed.

I agree wholeheartedly that every person has a role to play and that all levels of management should understand how their actions impact clients. My concern was not about the comment itself, but the fact that that the regulator felt the need to point this out to firms. Leaving aside conduct for a moment, business leaders should already know the value that middle management added and should have been ready to explain how it hadn't been overlooked; to management, this should never have been a blind spot.

I were part of that middle management, I might have taken it badly if my leadership decided to address me not because they acknowledged the value that I add but because the regulators had pointed out a need to do so. If firms spent significant effort reacting to this comment, in my view, that may indicate leadership sloppiness or a potential lack of understanding, not of conduct, but of their own business. When firms decided to implement good conduct, they should have assessed their needs across the organisation — looking carefully from analysts to senior managers, including in-house teams and suppliers. Needs would include training and other forms of day-to-day reinforcement to deliver a true change in culture, because if behaviours are not in alignment with training, training could give rise to a culture of cynicism or passive acceptance at best. Lack of fully thought-through solutions could add confusion, complexity and rework – all of which should be avoided.

With the global environment demanding more agile and effective solutions, we would be wise to articulate what we are trying to remedy before we set off.

Let's look at a related non-banking story to understand this point. Sky News reported that National Health Service (NHS) redundancy payoffs amounted to nearly £2bn during the government's restructuring programme over five years to 2015. However, more than 5,500 of those made redundant since 2010 were reemployed elsewhere in the NHS, despite some receiving severance payments of more than £200,000. The Shadow Health Secretary said that this was 'a reorganisation that didn't need to happen.'[viii]

That is precisely what I mean by high stakes. As an industry, before we embark on large programmes costing millions, we should take some time to bottom out where we want to go and what success looks like. Large budgets without clear goals would only result in large amounts being spent to get somewhere, only to realise that it may not be somewhere you wanted to go in the first place. Firms could look to explore more creative solutions, some of which we will explore later in the section on getting into the beat.

Fierce and competitive environment

I once saw an advert for a money exchange site called WeSwap which read, 'Why go to a banker for your travel money when you could go to fisherman?' Another similar advert read, 'Why go to a banker for your travel money when you could go to an art student?' The website read, 'WeSwap Travel Money – Exchange currency the new way and pay up to 10 times less than at banks, bureaux and airports.'

Going back to the film *Daddy Day Care*, the director of the exclusive Chapman Academy which had driven competitors out of business first dismissed Charlie as a fly-by-night operation, deriving comfort from the fact that she sold structure, discipline and five languages, only to admit much later, when it was too late, that 'He's selling fun. We can't compete with fun.' In the same vein, new organisations may have the ability to provide banking services with simpler features and access on the go that may appeal to the consumers of the future.

As companies get more creative with Big Data,[11] using it to deliver great insight, they are also going to be better at fraud prevention as they use customers' geolocation for physical whereabouts in addition to traditional proof of address documentation. Efficient and effective working is paramount at this moment and disruptive technologies should not be ignored but leveraged as best as possible. Traditional organisations need to focus on maximising key strengths, using them as solid foundations as they explore technological enhancements as opposed to letting past systems and failures bog them down, creating an air of panic, fear and burden capable of drowning agility.

What motivates people to come into work is that they make significant contribution to a visible and worthy goal; and not that over the course of a day, they may take one step forward in a marathon that could take years to finish, by which time the goalposts might have shifted anyway.

Potential bank exits

In May 2015, in the wake of increased regulation, HSBC announced that it was considering a move out of the UK – potentially back to its historical home in

---

[11] Big Data is a broad term for data sets so large or complex that traditional data processing applications are inadequate (Wikipedia).

Hong Kong. The move was followed by confirmed dialogue with Chinese regulators, though later in 2015, the bank's chairman, Douglas Flint, hinted that it could stay in the UK.[ix] Whether or not the bank moves will depend on many more factors, but the fact that it considered a move says a lot about the added pressure.

In a similar story, in May 2015, National Australia Bank revealed its Clydesdale demerger plan.[x] It had previously stated that it was considering options to pull out of the UK market because the misconduct charges were beginning to hurt. A further £1.7bn was to be provided to cover against potential costs of misconduct and mis-selling.

Earlier, in 2013, Clydesdale was charged £8.9 million for its treatment of customers affected by mortgage repayment errors, and then another £21 million in 2015 for failing to handle mis-selling claims properly. Clydesdale had discovered an error in how it had calculated mortgage repayments for customers with variable-rate mortgages and approximately 22,000 accounts were left with shortfalls. When the error was corrected, customers faced consequences such as unexpected increases in their monthly repayments or mortgage balances higher than they should have been, with shortfalls ranging from under £20 to over £18,000. The ruling states that after discovering the error, Clydesdale contacted customers and set up a dedicated call centre to deal with any queries. However, in seeking repayment from customers as a priority, it wrongly sought to balance its own commercial interests against the requirement to treat customers fairly.

On a slightly separate point, this story explains how poor conduct may well be a chain of events with discussions spanning the issue itself to the causal factors and remediation efforts, and may well include a set of people and teams as opposed to one team or the act of a single culpable person. We have discussed one school of thought, which suggested that conduct is all things people-related and should therefore be driven by Human Resources teams; this example should help clarify the narrowness of that understanding. Conduct may well be all things concerning people, process, technology, or any combination of these, and no one team can be tasked with getting it right. While business heads should be accountable, getting it right is everyone's responsibility. Suggesting that conduct is someone else's job is like suggesting that schools should take full accountability for moulding our children into responsible adults and that the healthcare services should take full responsibility for all health issues.

Coming back to exits, the fines may be necessary. From what I understand, in the UK FCA context, they are calculated using the penalty regime that the FCA applies to breaches committed after 6 March 2010; this was introduced in part to increase fine levels. My purpose is not to comment on the appropriateness of the fines or the handling of issues; my endeavour is only to join the dots: error, caused by poor decisions or failures in process or technology, followed potentially by poor handling of error, followed by punishment, eventually followed by players leaving or threatening to leave. Which might be better, to alter the punishment regime or perhaps continue until all bad players either get in line or leave? I believe that hard-hitting fines have caused firms to make some real changes, but wonder if change driven by fear of punishment is sustainable.

Increasing anxiety

For those still in the system, there is a need to ensure that we have a motivated workforce that looks forward to meeting the company's objectives, not one driven by fear of penalties and engulfed in shame and embarrassment as a result of past mistakes.

To quote some recent conversations, an elderly manager I met at a financial services conference said to me, 'I used to say I'm a banker, but now I just say I'm a civil servant.'

PwC and the London Business School conducted a research study, 'Stand Out for the Right Reasons: Why You Can't Scare Bankers Into Doing the Right Thing',xi to investigate the role of emotions in determining when and why employees behave creatively as opposed to unethically when competing with colleagues.

According to the PwC website, 'the report, based on a study of 2,431 managers from UK financial services organisations representing banking, insurance and wealth management, reveals that when presented with situations where the negative consequences or punishment for poor performance were highlighted, managers were 15% more anxious than excited, leading them to be more than twice as likely to behave unethically. Managers presented with the same situations, but with the positive outcomes of success highlighted, were correspondingly more excited, leading them to be more than twice as likely to demonstrate innovative behaviour.'

Duncan Wardley, people and change director and behavioural science specialist at PwC, said, 'We are not suggesting that rules and penalties for bad behaviour should be abandoned as it's essential that people know what is acceptable and what isn't, and criminal behaviour should be punished. This is about the sorts of pressures that push ordinary, well-meaning people into behaving less ethically that they would want to by cutting corners and hiding mistakes.'

I am testament to this dying excitement because, when I tell people that my book is about conduct, even the most genuine friends express reluctance to buy another book that will tell them how to behave. 'A book on conduct?' And I get a polite smile.

Giving into temptation

In *The Honest Truth about Dishonesty*, Dan Ariely pointed out what happens to the human mind when it is tired. Using the example of when we have had a really long hard day (moving day), Dan points out that on stressful days, many of us give in to temptation and succumb to the less healthy alternatives. This is backed by research demonstrating how we give into temptation when a part of our deliberative thinking is otherwise preoccupied.

Ariely explained this phenomenon by citing that that in his many years of teaching, there seemed to be an increase in deaths among close relatives of the students the closer it got to the end of the semester – usually a week before final exams and when papers were due.

There is thus an on-going struggle between the

impulsive and the rational parts of the human mind, which has a bearing on our decisions.

I wonder if all the remediation and energy put into cleaning behaviour may have a reverse impact, in that by placing people in environments of high distrust and tiredness levels, and making things increasingly difficult as we go, we may load rational brains to a tipping point where impulse takes over. While issues need to be addressed, how we address them is just as important as what we address.

As humans, we don't like the unknown and, while writing this book, I too was advised to play safe and focus on providing solutions because people are in a rush for answers and nobody wants more questions. It appears to me that in this rush to find the answers to the crisis, we have chosen to go for the simplest possible explanation – blaming the bankers.

From a compelling desire to identify the root cause (bankers' insatiable greed) and a rush to resolve this (more training and more regulation), I wonder if we may be guilty of 'boxing',[12] thereby increasing sustained pressure on many innocent people and driving them to do things that their rational minds might deem inconceivable – or simply forcing them

---

[12] Boxing is term commonly used when we generalise and categorise people into imaginary 'boxes', e.g. all Indians are vegetarians. Or in this case, all bankers are cheats.

to tune out to the point that they don't want to take any risks at all.

8. What conduct dilemmas look like in practice

We have already covered a few events that have arisen due to poor judgement and seen some stories that have led to fines, but we haven't yet looked at conduct dilemmas in the run-up to underlying decisions that result in such mistakes. Good conduct is very proactive in that that we actually consider the impact of our decisions before we make them. Conduct-related issues can often finds their root in business strategy because the strategy is the engine that drives day-to-day decisions.

Let's work this through a simple story.

Imagine you run a cake shop; let's call it Neetz. The banner reads, *Neetz – fresh homemade cakes since 1927*. It is a family run business that you inherited, and you are now the sole owner running the business with no help. Your shop is popular with locals.

Keeping your ears to the ground

People like the cakes, but sales have continued to drop, possibly due to competition and lifestyle changes. Life seems to go on, but you feel you may be on the verge of a burn-out. Lately, children have been stopping by asking for sweets – they appear to be children from a new school in the area. Little worries keep you awake at night; let's just call them the risks:

What if you fall ill? If you fell ill, the shop would not open. Customers might be disappointed and lose trust in the business, causing further strain.

What if profits continued to fall? You are barely breaking even and could easily go out of business. Overall, your business just doesn't look sustainable, and something needs to be done. You're not particularly excited about making changes, and shaking things up will be worrisome. However, just as there is a risk of doing something, there is the risk of doing nothing – you can't just sit and watch the business fall apart.

This isn't an unreal scenario. As more and more customers rely on sites such as Alibaba, Amazon and eBay, retailers are having to rethink strategies in the face of changing customer preferences. There are patterns even within online sales; more than a fifth of Britain's online sales take place on commuter journeys, for example, with spending totaling £9.3bn every year.[xii] Organisations need to be able to adapt to these patterns just to survive.

Right at the heart of conduct is your ability to observe these changes while continuing to care –yes, I know, care is a very soft word, but it's your business to care about your business, determining when something is not quite right, reading into something that others cannot, and finding patterns that may not be obvious to others. There are questions to be asked constantly: what are the sales telling you about buyer behaviour; what are your customers telling you; what else is going on in the city, and in the world; is there an opportunity as dynamics evolve; is there a threat that needs to be acted upon?

Once we have seen that something needs to be done, it is up to us to conduct ourselves in line with the responsibility entrusted in us. Whatever our business, whatever role we play in life, there will always be something that we can and cannot do. Covey captures the thought as he differentiates between the circle of influence and the circle of concern, whereby the circle of influence relates to things we can influence while the rest are things we can be concerned about but are limited in our ability to influence. More proactive thinking may normally mean more options, as we are likely to be able to act and not just react. What are your concerns, and which of these can you influence? Depending upon our make-up, i.e. our attitude towards life, we could choose to feel victimised by the changes, focusing on what we can't do, or we could be thinking of all the new things that we can do, feeling tremendously excited about new options and opportunities.

Determining the options

Just as critical as finding the patterns is the acknowledgment of what we find and the ability to take appropriate action. Our conduct will usually be evident in how we work through these options to determine our choices; and how much we compromise on ethics along the way. When faced with similar issues, our decisions will vary depending upon who we are – identical issues with identical challenges will still result in different actions.

Bearing this in mind, let's go back to our story and chalk out options for Neetz.

1. **You could start to stock readymade cakes.**
   Benefit: This will help to reduce costs and will save you time and effort.
   Risk: People may not like readymade cakes as much as the homemade ones. You might have to change the banner that advertises the cakes as homemade.
2. **You could stock candies for the school kids.**
   Benefit: This could give you the extra income with minimal additional effort.
   Risk: The children's parents may not like unhealthy food being sold to their children. While it is not a direct risk to you, it may impact your image in the community.

3. Hire help?
   Benefit: This will alleviate a lot of your stress.
   Risk: You just cannot afford this unless you supplement income or reduce costs.
4. Sell the business?
   Benefit: This would bring an instant benefit and reduce your financial exposure.
   Risk: Emotionally, you don't feel ready to walk away just yet. Your customers will need to seek alternatives.

There are many options. Usually, it is up to a few leaders to make the choice and for their teams to provide the insight to inform decisions. Our conduct and the appropriateness of it will be determined not just by the choice we make but also by the process we go through in arriving at that choice. Let's take a look at some considerations.

Making decisions

Ready-made cakes?

You may choose to stop selling homemade cakes all together. There is no problem with the decision. If you were to do this, the right thing to do would be to stop signposting homemade cakes. Alternatively, you could let the banner stay and hope that customers won't realise. But that would be just wrong, and risky as you might get into trouble if there were complaints. One way to get around this may be to stock just a small selection of homemade cakes in order to justify the banner. That way you won't feel like an outright fraudster and you could escape mis-selling allegations.

Something for the children?

What about bringing in something to attract the children? Cheap sugary sweets could give you an instant profit boost; something you desperately need. You may like to consider a slightly healthier variation such as sweets with high fruit content that make up one-a-day, or even sandwiches? That way you could support parents seeking healthy options. It would also work well for your image in the community as your objectives could become the same as those of the parents – to keep the children happy and healthy.

In a nutshell, these are the finer points where conduct comes in – because decisions are not made in isolation and options are not always black or white. Conduct is all things black and all things white thrown at you, and you having to choose that perfect shade of grey – the options may not be as many as 50, yet decision-making could be a daunting experience.

While our decisions are unique to us, they speak of how we conduct ourselves and our business. Beside the decision itself, it is the approach and the thinking that speaks of our conduct. Demonstrating good conduct is a bit like our math homework where we get marks for each step and not just the answer – because the magic sits those workings.

You may wonder what this has to do with conduct and judgment in the financial world. The underlying dilemmas relating to financial products and services are more complex but fundamentally similar in nature. A misleading banner is similar to confusing product brochures or hidden terms and conditions. Selling cheap sugary sweets to children may be similar to enticing vulnerable customers into decisions that may not be in their best interest. When organisations make these day-to day decisions, their conduct is clearly visible to the keen eye. Whether they make a conscious choice to consider conduct or it happens by default, there will always be conduct consideration, or lack of it.

One of the most common myths about conduct seems to be that spending more time talking about conduct is the same as practising good judgement. While focused effort may be an enabler, I suspect that you will find a correlation. Somewhat like when 15 minutes of time spent with a partner can be more powerful than hours of disengaged togetherness; or when 30 minutes of a good workout could be more effective than hours at the gym. What is more important is that conversations result in good judgement and subsequent action – a good fitness plan is a start, but you still need to put in the hard yards.

'Conduct is all things black and all things white thrown at you, and you having to choose that perfect shade of grey.'

Vinita Ramtri

> 'Rock bottom is good solid foundation to begin your climb.'

Anonymous

9. Getting on the beat

The best way to understand my stance would be that as the industry picks up the conduct beat, I see the benefits, yet I also see gaps. I see some very good intent and action, yet feel sometimes that several actions are merely about coping without really taking the time to think through and adapt. Simply recognising the need for change or preaching will not uplift behaviour, but neither will adding layers of complexity. Reinstating good conduct will be a case of getting into the beat and staying with it.

In April 2013, Liverpool football club striker Luis Suarez bit Chelsea defender Branislav Ivanovic. He was heavily criticised and there were jokes all over social media. It was clearly a case of poor behaviour and Suarez later confirmed that he had apologised directly to Ivanovic. His behaviour was appalling and worthy of punishment and he paid a penalty, served his bans and suspensions and eventually got back into the game. Does it need to be more complicated than that?

We need more positivity to get the economy, the

banks and our lives back on track – and we are amazingly good at it too. When smokers give in to the temptation of smoking, we assist them. When obesity becomes a national epidemic, we support the cause. Now that bankers have given into temptation, we need to call upon that same solution orientation. It is a very weak moment in a person's life when they rob someone of their livelihood, whatever the reason – greed, cutting corners or getting sloppy with governance. In many cases such as that of the US subprime lending or even PPI, the consequences were so far removed from the situation and that people may have not realised the gravity of their actions until it all blew up.

By adding more pressure on to the system, might we be making it that little bit worse by fatiguing people into further wrongdoing? If we wait with bated breath to hear of the next big failure, that's exactly what we will get to hear. In light of everything we have understood about conduct and the current world, it is incumbent upon us to dig deeper and find ways to get on the beat.

What we really need is more informed customers, less blame; more pride, less shame; more confidence, less fear; more encouragement, less punishment; more practitioners and fewer policemen. More doers and fewer checkers. More coaches, more mentors, more tools, more training.

In the rest of this book, we will explore some ideas and solutions.

Now, let's step into the arena.

'It is not the critic who counts; not the man who points out how the strong man stumbles, or where the doer of deeds could have done them better. The credit belongs to the man who is actually in the arena, whose face is marred by dust and sweat and blood; who strives valiantly; who errs, who comes short again and again, because there is no effort without error and shortcoming; but who does actually strive to do the deeds; who knows great enthusiasms, the great devotions; who spends himself in a worthy cause; who at the best knows in the end the triumph of high achievement, and who at the worst, if he fails, at least fails while daring greatly, so that his place shall never be with those cold and timid souls who neither know victory nor defeat.'

'Citizenship in a Republic'
Speech by the former President of the United States Theodore Roosevelt

10. Establishing the need

First things first; why should we care about correcting behaviour? We need to ask ourselves, whose need is it after all?

Waiting for regulation to tell us that we need to become proactive is, in my view, a very reactive way to become proactive. Regulation has its place, but the first big favour that firms can do for themselves is to stop seeing conduct as a 'requirement' that they need to abide by only to satisfy regulators. It would also serve well for us to shake ourselves out of the victim mentality of 'something that is being done to the firms'. The first step is the mindset.

Firms need to understand that having the right behaviours is in their interest just as much, if not more, as it is in the interest of the regulators or society as a whole.

There needs to be a genuine desire to want to do this right – not because we may be subject to regulatory visits but because it's the right thing to do and it makes perfectly good business sense if we are interested in running a sustainable business over the long-term. Here below are some really simple ways to test this mindset as it stands currently.

Confirming your stake

Leaders need to ask themselves whether they are invested in an organisation's wellbeing or are in for a quick profit. If they are leading an organisation, they need to be the former space and if they are not, it might be an option to consider ways to get more involved because they owe it to an organisation to be invested – I don't mean financially but emotionally.

Doing a SWOT

Here is one way to put your thinking to test. Do a SWOT analysis of the organisation scribbling spontaneously its key strengths, weaknesses, opportunities and threats as you see them. You may want to consider some things such as, a loyal customer base, low client attrition, your strategy, the culture etc.

Strengths   Weaknesses

Opportunities   Threats

Figure 1: SWOT Analysis

Once you have populated this, step back and see where you've written the customer and conduct-related items. If you see them as threats, it would appear to me that these items have been considered too late in the day and only addressed under the threat of a fine or regulatory action. It could also mean that items that you could otherwise consider to be opportunities are being seen as threats; for example, we may decide to improve how we handle complaints not because we want to serve people better but because there is new regulatory guidance around complaint handling.

These are very tiny points, and the exercise is a simple one, but what seems like a small transition from the right to the left is in fact a huge change in mindset and, in my view, an intangible yet key differentiator. I hope you will be able to make a conscious effort to move things around, untapping opportunities as you play to your strengths, because that's the arena where positive change happens.

Let's finish this thought with an example. You are sitting by the water and you see two people out for a run. They seem so similar in fitness and pace that you cannot tell if one is in a better state than the other. It's very cold and you wonder what their motivation is.

You stop them and ask, 'What motivates you to get

out of bed and on to the beach?'

The first says that having undergone extreme stress, his cholesterol is now high and the doctors have mandated exercise. Continued lack of exercise would be a threat to his life. He has no choice but to do something about it. The other person says that he is running because he loves to run, it keeps him fit and ready to take on life – getting a few minutes of run time in a busy life was an irresistible opportunity that just had to be seized.

That was two people doing the same activity but for two very different reasons, and that's what makes all the difference in how situations are handled and opportunities explored. It is true at an individual level, at an organisational level or even at a global level. When it comes to conduct, it is this thinking that will make the difference in how cultures will be embedded and incentives determined. Individuals and organisations should first take a moment to ask themselves why they care, and then take it from there.

It's perfectly possible that some of us may decide that we don't actually care and only want to do the bare minimum, just enough to avert the threat of regulatory action. If we were to realise that this is the case, it might be time to think about what really does motivate us, and if we are in the right business after all.

In summary, as individuals and as organisations, we need to be clear whether conduct really matters to us, or whether we make it matter because we have been asked to make it matter.

'Purpose and positioning first,

Client profiling second,

Business, and conduct, will follow.'

Vinita Ramtri

11. Getting the focus right

There was a strange incident that engulfed Indians (particularly Hindus) globally in 1995. I'm an eyewitness to this story. One September morning, we woke up to the news that statues of Ganesha, the Indian elephant-headed god, were drinking milk. Worshippers claimed that when they held up milk to the elephant's trunk, it was seen to disappear; apparently the idol was drinking milk. It was totally bizarre, but word spread quickly, and devotees all over India and beyond – in the UK, Canada, UAE and Nepal – bought into the miracle, and milk sales in Delhi alone were reported to have jumped by about 30% for that one day. There were queues spilling out of temples causing traffic mayhem.

The astonishing thing was that while milk flowed down the drains, poor children still slept hungry. People prioritised getting milk to the idol over giving it to the poor. We, as a society, had the capacity to help the poor – because we had milk supply and purchasing power. We also saw ourselves as a community of good, godfearing citizens – which is evident from the fact that people bought milk and queued for hours just to offer it to their deity. We had all the makings to do the right thing and yet, the focus, in my view, was slightly misdirected.

Perhaps the masses wanting to please God may not have asked themselves if God might be perfectly happy for His share of milk to be given to the poor. Sometimes, to achieve an aim, we need to aim at the bull's eye, but often this may not be the case.

When it comes to good conduct, I believe, we need to focus less on the regulation and more on clients, the people who serve these clients, the processes that lend themselves to enabling better service, the technology that allows people to provide a better experience and all those little things in between. These then come together to give you the happy Ganesha.

Firms that don't understand this could find themselves ignoring fundamental business priorities such as increasing complaints, workload queues and employee frustration while spending valuable time and resource on potentially insignificant deliverables with short-lived benefits. Adopting an approach to focus merely on guidance could result in firms becoming one-trick ponies who find themselves subject to constantly shifting focus, and never really being able to develop their own style. Such firms must not kid themselves that they are leaders because at best, they may be good followers or good copies and will be only ever be better than those living in denial or oblivion.

The firms that really stand out will be the ones who define the right focus for their organisation, while also establishing why good conduct is good for them. These are the firms that will generate examples for the others to follow.

To run after every new trend, not because you believe in it, not because it aligns with your purpose and not because it is the answer to your issues, but because that's what everyone will be doing, is not good for any firm. Firms need to be very clear on their purpose so they don't spend precious resource on red herrings. Here are some risks that come with the copycat approach.

1. Generating false positives: These are often called type 1 errors or Alpha errors and refer to a test result that generates false positives. In practice, when this happens, we may like a process or an approach and, without taking the time to assess how the solution is good for our business, we may just get on the bandwagon to get a piece of the pie;

potentially pulling apart something that was working perfectly well to get a solution that just doesn't work for us. You may be able to recall examples of when something that was working well was replaced by a solution not so ideal, only so that we could revert to the original. If not in your organisation, I am sure we have seen this in other walks of life; like when you paint a wall blue only to paint it white again, or when you buy a posh car, only to realise that you miss the previous comfort drive. What I refer to here are not genuine mistakes or just the side-effects of evolution, but knee-jerk proposals in response to misguided focus usually driven by what everyone else was doing.

2. Chaos and confusion: Constantly changing priorities will at first cause some unrest. If this is allowed to run long enough, people adapt and develop apathy and just stop caring. That's when you have the real issue – a disengaged workforce that will just plod along; in the case of the milk episode, they would queue without even asking why.

3. Leadership credibility: Leaders could risk losing credibility if their initiatives or decisions appear to be knee-jerk reactions and pet projects start to feel like 'flavour of the month' as opposed to well thought-through statements worth aspiring to.

Employee surveys indicating lack of confidence in leadership decisions or sense of pride in working for an organisation may be indicators, but of course you would need to analyse this further against other variables at play.

Would it not be better to look inside out, beginning with understanding your own purpose of existence and then aligning everything else to this purpose? There are clear advantages with this approach.

1. Single purpose: Firms that use this approach can continue to be focused on their business, its purpose and its customers, and still be right in conduct as opposed to trying to retro-fit conduct into their already defined objectives. Conduct needs to be woven into core objectives so that client interest is the firm's interest. These are the firms that will continue to prosper in the future.

2. No added effort: If your purpose is aligned to client interest, effort spent on achieving a business objective is effort spent on good conduct. Firms would then just need to continue to work towards their objectives and they would be practising good conduct by default.

3. Belief: Most importantly, employees begin to feel the synchronisation. If employees leave

meetings and training sessions feeling that they are all moving in the same direction, there is a certain sense of belonging and group momentum that is hard to define in tangible terms. A clear alignment of messages takes away unnecessary stress that may be created by conflicting priorities. When training objectives are not aligned to performance incentives, for example, this could create an internal conflict: I am being taught to do one thing but rewarded for doing another.

To conclude, getting the focus right and keeping it consistent is paramount as it will define the flow of energy. Constantly changing focus can disrupt this flow and erode credibility. People choose leaders just as much as leaders choose their people. Anyone can become a manager by hierarchy, but for teams to want to listen to what leaders have to say, they have to establish credibility by giving them something worth listening to and a goal worth pursuing.

The day that firms realise that they need to have the same personal objectives as their clients,[xiii] they should not have to worry about changing focus to suit conduct, because when clients hurt, they will hurt too. The only thing better than aligned objectives is to have the same objectives.

12. Recognising multiple start points

Conduct risk is a new concept and was only introduced by the FCA towards the end of 2013. The concept is more mature in the UK and America, but is moving into other regions. Given its infancy, combined with the urgency of resolving it, it is common practice for firms to seek conduct experts to help them land this behavioural change and meet regulatory expectations.

In doing so, we need to be careful not to undermine existing employees who may have been practising great conduct over many years. High-performing and well engaged teams may have reached a point where they don't feel the need to explain conduct considerations because that would be stating the obvious and a waste of time.

This may be better understood using the model explaining the four levels of competence. The model explains any learning process where we graduate from being unaware of a skill (unconscious incompetence) to being so adept at it that we practise it without making a conscious effort (unconscious competence).

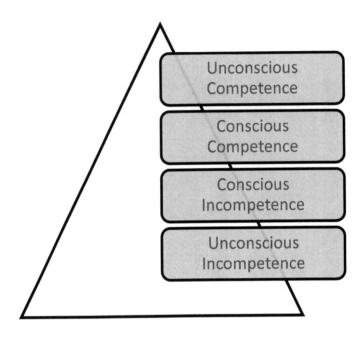

Figure 2: Levels of Competence

Let's take the example of learning to drive:

1. Unconscious Incompetence: We don't know what we don't know. We aren't born with the ability to drive but we didn't know any better.
2. Conscious Incompetence: We realise that there is a skill that we don't possess. By the age of four or five, we may come to realise that driving is a skill that we don't have. This is when children start asking when they can learn how to drive and if it is easy or hard.
3. Conscious Competence: We learn a new skill and use it carefully. Assuming that we choose

to learn to drive, we take lessons and while we are new at this, we drive with conscious awareness so that we notice every turn and every change in gear.

4. Unconscious Competence: We use the skill without realising that we are using it. As we drive for an extended periods of time, we come to a point where we drive around with such ease and spontaneity that we can talk and listen to music at the same time and not take note of every gear change.

The same goes with walking, eating and many other skills that we acquire. The reason I cite this in the context of conduct is that many employees may be at the final stage, the level four, where they practise good conduct without realising this or taking credit for it each time they do so. They just do the right thing and don't think it necessary to tell anyone. It is when these employees are asked to start to evidence good conduct that it causes confusion.

Lacking evidence could be a misleading symptom

People make decisions for various reasons. While the decisions are communicated, the rationale is not always repeatedly reinforced, particularly when there is a high degree of trust and experience in the group. For example, technology teams may decide to deploy a patch to fix some defects but might not necessarily document the exact reasons for prioritisation. I may tell my child that I need her to do certain things such as complete her homework, eat a healthy meal and make sure she gets to school on time, etc., but I may not always follow up with the rationale that I say all this because I care for her wellbeing. You might tell a partner you want to see them for dinner not bothering to explain that it is because you love spending time with them.

When observing decisions made from day-to-day meetings all the way up the hierarchy, we need to appreciate the fact that when we see no clear evidence of how conduct has been considered, we could be dealing with someone who lacks client concern; but equally, we could be dealing with someone who is very aware of good conduct but does not see the need to explain their rationale.

Leaders and practitioners thus need to acknowledge that symptoms could be misleading in that the absolute lack of conduct considerations or extreme recognition of conduct both may look the same and may mean that we won't be speaking of conduct any more. Now let's take a look at why this matters.

Adapting your training approach

Because of previous wrongdoing and conduct being a new principle, consultants and trainers may often begin with the assumption that everyone needs to be taught from level one, as if no one understands anything about doing the right thing. They often dive straight into statistics regarding fines in the hope that the staggering figures and the resulting sense of shame may contribute to a punchy pitch.

When this approach is applied to those at level one, who are just starting out, the fear could get anchored and define their orientation to conduct for years to come. Those at a level four, on the other hand, may get confused about where they went wrong or find the training patronising. Alternatively, we may sometimes choose not train anyone, and simply impose additional controls and reporting requirements without providing the necessary context. Hence, the training approach being that that there is no need for additional training. This too could be a cause for frustration because we are in a way asking for people to get to level three where decisions are carefully articulated without fully recognising that everyone is at a different start point. Such solutions may work in the short-term but will seldom stick because people would have been forced to the 'what' without explaining the 'why' and may view the new requirements as noise, added burden or increased bureaucracy; or worse; something that is being done just to please the regulators.

In summary, conduct training approach needs to be flexible enough to respect and acknowledge people at both ends of this spectrum so that committed employees don't feel humiliated by assumptions that they know nothing of a talent they display every day, while trainers repeatedly use terms such as 'I don't want to teach you to suck eggs' though that's precisely what they may be doing. Additionally, there is the need to go beyond the 'what' into the 'why' as it will definitely help teams get increased buy-in, creating steeper learning curves with learning that sticks. When I say why, I refer to a positive sense of purpose and not to the threat of fines and regimes.

In my view, training should be basic, moving quickly from the purpose into creative, day-to-day decisions and dilemmas so that people have the opportunity to understand how this applies to their role as opposed to having to sit multiple lessons on morals and values.

Adapting to the future

The tricky part here is that while level four is a great place to be, your end goal is to find that sweet spot between levels three and four because firms should get accustomed to maintaining evidence trails, ideally with no added effort. Those who believe that they should be trusted to make the right decisions without being answerable to anyone need to recognise that it's in the organisation's long-term interest that there be a decent evidence trail – a little effort today can save a lot of pain for future leaders. This is not about lack of trust but just good stewardship. Just as we have this planet to enjoy and yet we need to realise that future generations will pay the price for our misuse.

Beside the bit to learn, there are a few careless practices to unlearn. This process of unlearning and relearning reminds me of a time when I came to the UK and had to get a driving license. Having driven around India for 10 odd years, it felt awkward to be signing up for driving lessons. My instructor explained that I wasn't there to learn to drive, but to learn to drive the UK way, and that I was going to have to unlearn and relearn. I later realised that I had picked up a few bad habits along the way, so it's not such a bad thing to unlearn every once in a while – somewhat like a detox after wild partying.

Wearing the client hat

Satya Bansal, the CEO of Barclays Wealth India, suggested that a good way to apply conduct thinking in everyday decisions is to appoint a person to wear the client hat, inspired by Edward De Bono's concept of the six thinking hats. How this works in practice is that at key meetings and decision-making sessions, one of the leaders would be represent the client; hence the name client hat. Their primary role would be to evaluate every discussion from a client standpoint, possibly expressing delight, raising questions, or concerns, as real customers would do.

For example, if the marketing manager was appointed as the customer for a meeting where the business was introducing a new mobile app, some questions that he might ask would be, 'How will I know about the app? Can I use this on my iPad? Where will I find log-in details? What happens if it does not recognise my credentials? Why will I want to use it? Whom can I contact if the app crashes or kicks me out mid-session? Can my wife and I log in simultaneously as we have a joint account? Will it cost anything? Do you have a training video on how to use this app? Can I leave feedback on the app?'

Satya said it was a practice they used often and that it worked for them because not only was it more subtle, it was better integrated. I believe this is a great way of infusing client thinking into our discussions because of its sheer simplicity, and other merits including:

1. The entire team would begin to appreciate the client view as they listen to peers and also raise questions themselves when they take their turn to wear the client hat.

2. Since the responsibility rotates, no one person or department would be singled out as the expert or potentially the blocker.
3. Decisions would be better thought through helping teams downstream who execute these decisions, painstakingly writing detailed requirements and specifications.
4. We may need fewer meetings given that the agenda would be broad enough to include conduct therefore eliminating or reducing the need for separate discussions.

I believe that if we do this long enough, everyone will learn to appreciate the client view, and you may not even need to appoint anyone because there is a little bit of client in each one of us. An even better solution may be that everyone is actually a client and not just wearing a hat, but I realise that this may not always be possible.

13. Whose job is it anyway?

In an interview with Vishal Sikka, the CEO of Infosys,[xiv] he was asked about innovation in his organisation. He said, 'Innovation has to come from everybody. It has to come everywhere. And this is why I say, the Innovation Department in Infosys is Infosys.'

I mentioned before that conduct is pervasive in that everyone needs to be doing this all the time and that we have collective responsibility to do what is right by our firm and its customers.

Let's look at some practical ways to do this.

There is a lot of focus on the three lines of defence model. For those new to the term, it essentially means that people in the organisation are split into three types.

The first line of defence is the business, i.e. the people who interact with customers and support those who do, and these people are normally called the business. This line often bears the key accountability to do the right thing. The second is the compliance function, whose role it is to act as a coherent opposition, scrutinising all decisions and actions. Finally there is a third line that performs audit functions, flagging issues so that business can fix these. Simply put, business normally does the doing, and business heads normally include the business CEOs and COOs; the checkers do the checking; the auditors do the auditing. It is common to explain a role as 1LoD, 2LoD or 3LoD, where LoD means Line of Defence. Getting conduct and market behaviour right is usually the responsibility of the business, and rightfully so because the business owns the customer relationships – the rest of the roles, while crucial, are peripheral to that core relationship between clients and the business.

Getting creative with the Lines of Defence

When this comes down to everyday practice, it is similar to the client hat concept, in which business wears the accountability hat, while accountability may rotate within the first line but is usually not passed on to the second or third lines. People normally pick a role in any one line of defence and develop expertise within that role, e.g. auditors will usually audit while bankers will normally be bankers. It is possible but rare that people will go from becoming bankers to auditors or vice versa. Any exposure to another role is normally done by way of a formal secondment or a taster such as 'a day in the life of', in a way that makes it clearly distinguishable as an activity outside our daily role, usually undertaken for a specific reason.

I can't help feeling that this is all too linear and rigid, contributing to silo thinking so that no one role fully appreciates the role of the other line. With conduct being something that business is usually accountable for (though this may vary in some organisations), industry discussions indicate that businesses feel tremendously burdened as there is more to be done and more to be checked, while focus on shareholder returns and profitability doesn't fully go away either. Compliance functions have seen tremendous growth since the crisis, thereby suggesting more checks. The expectation normally is that while conduct is everyone's role, it is for the business to deliver, while compliance and audit functions ensure that it is being delivered right.

Taking a new spin on this, we all know that the naughtiest children make the best class monitors. We also know that working in silos is not a good thing. Why then do we not get a bit more creative with our structures, finding ways to allow for some cross-fertilisation between the three lines? Have you ever wondered what it may be like if the doers could check the work of peers and if the checkers became the doers for a while? For checkers, it is important to understand the challenges of the role in addition to the rules, and for the doers they may be able to contribute a lot to the checking system because they may know exactly where the gaps are.

This story should help to validate the above point. Frank Abagnale was an American fraudster and the subject of the 2002 film *Catch Me if You Can*, starring Leonardo DiCaprio. Forty years ago, Abagnale cashed in forged cheques worth more than $2.5 million. Before he reached the age of 18, he had already posed as a pilot, a lawyer, a professor and a pediatrician – and got away with it. When he was eventually jailed, the FBI recruited him to help catch others like him, which he has done for the past 35 years. As I write this book, he is in South Africa to consult on cybercrime and is a respected authority on forgery, embezzlement and secure documents.[xv]

There must be something we can learn from this. Could we perhaps consider more dynamic models where some days could be split between the three lines of defence? These may be some benefits to be derived:

1. We develop a better appreciation of each other's roles, potentially reducing the likelihood of individuals and functions blaming one another.
2. We gain a deeper understanding of all aspects of the business, e.g. business learns a bit more about the regulations that impact them while compliance understands more about how the daily challenges in a business and how regulations impact businesses.

The skill set may require some expansion, but not hugely because the doer, the checker and the auditor must all possess the same fundamental expertise such as retail banking, wealth banking, credit cards, mortgages etc. While not suggesting a one-third split between all the three lines of defence, a good governance model in my view would be one that allows everyone to experience, recognise and contribute to and learn from another person's role so that we begin to transition out of our silos; not by relying on individuals initiatives but by making it an integral part of the system – at least for a few key roles.

Finding new ideas

Perhaps besides implementing readymade innovative ideas presented to them, leaders need to get their hands dirty and generate some ideas from getting more skin in the game. The TV series *Undercover Boss* is a good example of how this could be done. In each series of the show, executives at large businesses go undercover posing as entry-level employees, coming away with new findings about their companies, the employees – their personal and professional challenges. In one of the episodes, Dan DiZio, CEO of the Philly Pretzel Factory, admits that you get caught in this web of this business... you get caught up in these meetings and don't get a chance to come out. And I believe that's symptomatic of many organisations; well-meaning people, just too caught up to see any different. What we need is for more CEOs to be getting their hands dirty to see how these lines of defence work in practice and more people spending time in each other's business areas.

As we all get comfortable in our roles and strive to do it to perfection, we get further removed from the others in the organisation, often collaborating not because we share a common goal but because we are required to so or even because we know that we will be assessed on others' opinions of us. Ironically, sometimes objectives are defined in such a way that we are almost at odds with one another, forgetting that there is a greater purpose. We will be able to see some examples of this when we discuss the differences between operational risk and conduct risk, and the need for a holistic risk management framework focused on resolution more than categorisation.

To summarise, common belief and common practice guard against thinking and living in silos and suggest that teams and organisations need to be better coordinated. Adapting operating models or job roles to allow for natural exposure to each other's roles could help enhance effectiveness in general. For conduct in particular, where businesses feel burdened by the added checks, this could be a solution worth trialling. For employees who seek more challenge, this thinking may offer additional benefits such as job expansion, eventually leading to broader skill-sets and wider networks, potentially resulting to a drop in attrition as lateral moves into other lines of defence might become realistic options.

'Although there is no right way to do the wrong thing, there are many ways you can do the right thing wrong.'

Vinita Ramtri

14. Changing how you change

As organisations need to evolve constantly just to stay relevant, change is the only constant. Change can come in many shapes and sizes, known, unknown, proactive, reactive, strategic, tactical, regulatory, mandatory, global, local – the list goes on. Whether businesses plan to change a product or service or something in the backend that customers can't really see but could be impacted by, such as changes to how organisations store their customers' data and who they share this with, they need to think through the client impact of change.

This should not be new to any change practitioner. Traditionally though, change has often been more focused on the impact on the firm as opposed to its impact on customers. Conduct doesn't change the methodology, it only broadens this focus to ensure that there is a more holistic assessment of the benefits and risks so we aren't just thinking of the business but also the customers.

As in the cake shop example, the customer

consideration would come in at various stages even before we accept the need for change all the way through to checking how well the change has been received. Let us look at this in stages, beginning with the purpose.

Getting the purpose right

As always, it starts with the purpose. Firms need to understand and be able to articulate the purpose for change by asking themselves what it is that they want to achieve through the change. And then the harder question, is that the right thing to be aiming for?

There is no right way to do the wrong thing. If the intent is negative, firms will only get so far before they will need to take a hard look at the objective. On the contrary, if the underlying intent is positive, minor slips in execution may be acceptable. This is essentially the 'Why' for doing anything, and is closely aligned to what your business stands for, e.g. profit through delivering positive changes to people's lives, or profit for its own sake regardless of its cost to society or the customers. Hopefully, we understand by now that wanting to make a profit or meeting shareholder expectations does not have to be at odds with good conduct. Shareholders want a good share value but also a brand that they would like to be associated with. When Volkswagen admitted to cheating, its shares plummeted by 35% in two trading days and the company was setting aside over $7.0 billion; estimating that cheating impacted 11 million cars.

Coming back to change, let's see some cases of change through the conduct lens.

The right strategy well executed: BSkyB

While working for BSkyB, the UK's leading entertainment provider, I was part of a programme working on parental controls for home broadband. This is at the heart of conduct because parents should be able to block their children from being exposed to inappropriate content. Being a different industry, there was no formal conduct banner and yet it in spirit, it has conduct written all over it. Let us look through how the conduct discussions might flow.

The purpose

Increase protection of children from exposure to inappropriate online content.

The strategy and objectives

To develop a product that would enable parents to determine what can and cannot be viewed for devices connected through the home Wi-Fi. Parents will be able to do this by adjusting router settings using their Sky iD. The product would be called Sky Broadband Shield.

The execution

At this point it gets trickier because there are many ways to fulfil the strategic objectives. There are finer nuances to be considered such as these:

- The product could be such that customers could to determine settings at a home level so that all devices work to the same setting or potentially enable customers to vary the settings by device, e.g. my iPhone may have different permissions to my child's iPad.
- There could be a limit to the number of times that customers could change the settings, e.g. two changes per month. Alternatively this could be unlimited or be done for a small fee.
- In terms of roll-out, new and existing customers could be informed on a one on one basis such using letters, email and texts and this could be supplemented with a marketing campaign.

When executing change, there are multiple decision points and options that need to be considered in the light of what is viable and how the decisions will impact customers.

As a Sky customer, I felt that the product was fairly useful. I found the parental control offering though my online account and options included family viewing, suitable for 13 and suitable for 18. My selection would take effect in minutes and I could make any number of changes any time I liked. A useful product that was fairly easy to use.

The right strategy with gaps in execution: DVLA

In a similar example, UK's Driving Vehicle Licensing Authority (DVLA) rolled out a change early in 2015 that is believed to have caused some client inconvenience. In the UK, a license normally had two parts: a plastic photocard driving license and a paper counterpart. It was decided that from the 8 of June 2015 the paper counterpart was to be replaced by an online service.[xvi] This change would save motorists money, reducing unnecessary red tape and putting license holders in control of their information, while sharing the most up-to-date information with third parties as required. What this change meant for users was that if we needed to share our details with a car hire company (assuming you were going on holiday) or employers, we would need to go to gov.uk and generate a check code. To generate the check code, we would need our driving license number, National Insurance (NI) number and postcode. The check code would then be valid for three days – I believe this was later revised to 21 days. This code could then be shared in multiple ways.

Strategically, it is a perfectly well-meaning change. But from reviews post the launch, it appeared that there were some gaps in the consideration of its impact on customers, some of whom may have suffered avoidable annoyance and inconvenience as a result. It appears that people travelling may not have known of the change before they travelled, and thus found themselves in awkward situations when trying to rent cars abroad. Regarding the details required to generate the check code, perhaps these could have been simpler and easier to remember, or something users could set up themselves.

To conclude, change is a key area that has the potential to cause customer inconvenience and distress. However, all the same, all development in the world depends upon change. It may even be that change that causes inconvenience is actually good for us; we will explore this in the chapter on conduct and customer experience. Firms must therefore view change positively, only making sure that when working through it they think of customers just as much as they think about themselves.

'Each day you are leading by example. Whether you realize it or not or whether it's positive or negative, you are influencing those around you.'

Rob Liano

15. Leadership dilemmas

Authentic leadership is the core of a good conduct culture. Not only do leaders need to be seen saying and doing the right thing, they need to take a moment to explain why they believe something is the right thing to do. The little added effort helps establish leadership credibility providing better engagement because employees have a chance of making a connection as opposed to taking something at face value.

In the context of conduct, the hard part about being a leader is that the leader's judgement is always being watched to set the tone of the organisation. Whether they use this judgement to start something, to refuse to start something, to stop something, to refuse to stop something, to do something or to do nothing, their decisions are being observed and learnt from – as an 'on-the-job' conduct training if you like. Even if they choose to jump off a sinking ship, all eyes will still be on them.

As we discussed in the chapter 'Getting to grips with conduct', it is common, particularly for leaders, to confuse poor conduct with culpable actions or wilful harm, i.e. active decisions intended to cause harm. Conduct responsibilities go much beyond that, though, as we will explore in this chapter. Leaders cannot be across everything and therefore a lot depends on both teams and leaders to bridge this gap.

As an example, at some technology events related to topics such as cyber resilience and Big Data, practitioners mentioned leadership buy-in as one of their key challenges, stating that they struggled to get their leaders over the line in these areas. Whether dealing with specific topics related to data storage in the cloud or additional investment in technology that would enhance data protection and cyber resilience, or just the introduction of banking alternatives like mobile banking, people believe that one of the biggest challenges is to help the CEOs get technology. Organisation must have the right framework to ensure that important issues come to light and that leaders are supported in making the right decisions.

And for the leaders today, we have mentioned before how important it is that they listen and have the courage and humility to put their hand up when they are not sure, if only to say, 'I think I need some help here', or 'I don't get it' and, when required, own up to their mistakes.

While the range of decisions and its justification is a vast topic that we have been exploring throughout the book, the reason conduct is so pertinent in a leader's role is that their judgement can have far-reaching consequences. We are all leaders in our own right, often making decisions that impact a wide range of people in multiple ways – be it by way of financials or non-financial aspects such as stress levels, lifestyle, education and other issues that may seem mundane to decision-making committees or boards. Leadership roles range from those granted to us explicitly by appointment to positions of power to those that are implicit in the nature of what we do.

When I say leaders in this book, I usually refer to CEOs and political personalities who have the ability to impact clients and markets. I also refer to celebrities, pilots and doctors who are in exceptionally trustworthy positions where thousands of people look up to them and families put their faith in them. There are more of us leading than we might care to acknowledge.

Recognising that there are more than just two options

At the start of the conduct debate, leaders seemed

to believe that they were accountable only at the point where they had actively taken action that had caused harm, and in other cases continued to plead that it wasn't something they had initiated or even knew anything about. As Lord Green and Bob Diamond came under fire for mistakes related to tax evasion and Libor when they held key positions, it became apparent that accountability for conduct would be broader than that. As with all conduct matters, the issue isn't limited to the financial sector. In the News International phone hacking scandal, the parliamentary select committee report concluded that Rupert Murdoch 'exhibited wilful blindness'.

Given that leaders' responsibilities extend beyond active decision-making into taking reasonable steps to ensure that poor behaviours are not incentivised and maybe even actively discouraged, I tried to make sense of all the combinations and have designed this framework to try and explain the various outcomes – good and bad leaders' options – such as taking an action or taking no action, and eventually the end assessment that determines whether that judgement call was a good move or a bad move. I have called it the Leadership Dilemma.

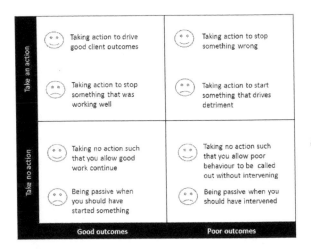

	Good outcomes	Poor outcomes
Take an action	Taking action to drive good client outcomes	Taking action to stop something wrong
	Taking action to stop something that was working well	Taking action to start something that drives detriment
Take no action	Taking no action such that you allow good work continue	Taking no action such that you allow poor behaviour to be called out without intervening
	Being passive when you should have started something	Being passive when you should have intervened

Figure 3: Leadership Dilemmas

Let's look at some examples to understand this.

A bad move: Take an action / Poor outcomes

In one of the worst shipping disasters of all time, Captain Francesco Schettino was found guilty of manslaughter and sentenced to 16 years in prison after his ship the *Costa Concordia* hit the rocks and sank in 2012, killing 32 people. Captain Schettino was accused of bringing his 290m-long vessel too close to shore when it struck rocks off the Tuscan island of Giglio, forcing over 4,000 passengers and crew into a chaotic evacuation. He was also charged with abandoning the ship, though his lawyers claimed that he fell into a lifeboat.

Schettino went on trial for multiple manslaughter and abandoning the ship. The court gave him 16 years for multiple manslaughter, causing the shipwreck, abandoning passengers and providing false information to port authorities.

In relation to the framework, the captain's move was a bad one in a way that he took an action that resulted in poor outcomes, although it wasn't planned with the intention of causing a disaster.

Bad move: Take no action / Poor outcomes:

In the case of the Clydesdale fine for £21 million mentioned earlier, the FCA stated that the bank's senior managers did not know what was happening, but it did have inappropriate procedures that stopped a proper search. In my view, this could be an example of failing to take an action, in this case to introduce appropriate procedures, which led to client harm —being passive when it may have been useful to intervene.

I have designed the diagram not to be used as a 'tick box' activity or a checklist, but as a framework to help broaden leaders' minds about the areas to explore and ultimately develop their own decision-making style as opposed to confining thinking to cases from the past.

In summary, judgement is a very broad word and therefore filled with dilemmas. As markets and behaviours undergo change, sometimes at tremendous velocity, the good and the great will be differentiated by the pace and finesse with judgement evolves – in teams, leaders, organisations and even economies.

'Risk comes from not knowing what you are doing.'

Warren Buffet

16. Being bold

Courage is a non-tradeable leadership trait and continues to gain even more relevance, largely because of the rate of change and increased pressure caused by ongoing scrutiny where almost every move we make could be on record and available for public examination.

When conduct challenges strike, they put every leadership skill to test, and it takes a great amount of internal strength to be able respond in a way that can retain trust and confidence amongst diverse stakeholders ranging from employees and shareholders to politicians and regulators.

This is especially true of conduct, because when right and wrong become a matter of opinion, solutions depend heavily on a leader's ability to determine the appropriate response in a timely manner, talking it through with anyone who needs to understand.

Let's take a look at leadership examples relating to conduct – some very bold and others not so bold.

Being bold enough to be transparent

It takes a lot of confidence to share information transparently, and often organisations may be caught in a culture of fear in which no one wants to be seen as the bearer of bad news.

Coming back to the story of the ship, when giving evidence to the trial, Captain Schettino was asked why he instructed his crew to tell passengers that the ship had simply experienced a power blackout and that they had nothing to worry about – a level of reassurance that meant some passengers stayed in their cabins and lost their lives when the ship went down. He said, 'I did that to calm the passengers down. I feared that otherwise there would be panic.'[xvii]

Sometimes, panic is not such a bad thing.

The same could be true of politicians. Some of the causes for the economic instability in August 2015 could be blamed on leaders avoiding tough decisions that may have been good in the long-term but would not be popular at the start. This could include Putin's resistance to liberalisation and privatisation and Brazil's reluctance to take on corruption. Such decisions require a lot of courage and may cost people their careers.

Leaders can sometimes be found putting off decisions and interactions, although that too is a position being carefully watched. People have the right to know just so they can make informed decisions – and leaders need to have the wisdom to determine what needs to be told to whom and when. When leaders avoid transparency, people feel cheated, not protected.

Being bold enough to apologise

Early in 2015, I read an open letter from social activists in India addressed to Aishwarya Rai Bachchan, a former Miss World, UNAIDS ambassador and a popular Bollywood star. Activists were enraged by a jewellery print advert for Kalyan jewellers that featured the star and an 'underage slave-child' holding a parasol. Entitled 'Open letter to Aishwarya Rai Bachchan: This ad you figure in is insidiously racist,' the letter read, 'In the advertisement you appear to be representing aristocracy from a bygone era – bejewelled, poised and relaxing while an obviously underage slave-child, very dark and emaciated, struggles to hold an oversize umbrella over your head.'

Key issues raised were that advertisements were a critical part of Indian society and that the advert could be seen to promote racism and child labour. The letter urged Aishwarya to cease to associate herself with the image and circulate a 'considered public retraction'.

Figure 4: The advert as it originally appeared

Subsequently, I saw another article where her publicist suggested that Aishwarya was not involved in the final image. Thanking the authors for drawing their attention to the perception of the advertisement, she attached a shot from the actual shoot.

Subsequently, Kalyan withdrew the advert, saying, 'This creative was intended to present royalty, timeless beauty and elegance. It we have, inadvertently, hurt the sentiments of any individual or organisation, we deeply regret the same.'

Figure 5: The advert as later clarified

While I have used true names and details to keep this real, my intention here is not to name and shame, but analyse events and behaviours to draw some learning in the context of the how leaders exercise the options available to them, the decisions they take and the resulting impact of these decisions. Transparency and prompt action are fundamental to conduct even when restoring damage. Both Aishwarya and Kalyan jewellers issued coordinated responses backed by action. From a mitigation perspective, everything appeared to be fairly well handled.

There are two more key points to note. Firstly, what we see may not always be true – the difference between the two images makes that clear. What seems like irresponsible behaviour may not have been so. Those in the arena should be able to explain and those watching the action should keep an open mind and seek the truth before they judge. Secondly, the larger the profile, the more the scrutiny. Smaller companies behaving unethically may get away more lightly than larger names who appear to carry greater responsibility in setting the tone in society. This is a slightly dangerous habit as we get accustomed to overlooking the many small warning signs until they become flashing lights. We will touch upon this when we come to metrics.

Being bold enough to continue

Let's look at another similar public debate again early in 2015. This one relates to a protein power advert that advert read, 'Are you beach body ready?' Protein World is an online fitness company and caused a Twitter storm with its advert featuring a model with a slim waist in a little yellow bikini. The advert sparked worldwide controversy over body shaming.

CEO Arjun Seth, who lives in London, is believed to be a walking advert of the product. The campaign continued and as far as Protein World was concerned, they said that the advert and the subsequent row helped them promote their true message, 'Get off your a** and do something about it'. It is believed that the row over the advert brought them an additional £2 million.

After several complaints to the Advertising Standards Agency (ASA), the advert was banned in the UK with the ASA launching investigations. While it was removed from the London Underground, it continued to feature at New York's Times Square. There are two sides to this argument. Whatever your view of the advert, the point I wish to explore is that Arjun Seth had to make a decision and he stuck by his team and his decision; no retractions and no apologies. It is that boldness that I find credible.

The two examples are so similar and yet so different. The Kalyan advert attracted attention just as Protein World did, and in both examples we saw action – one choosing to retract and apologise while the other chose to continue full force, moving on to other global destinations. One chose to apologise and the other stood its ground, accepting the risk of fallout.

To summarise, the right answer is that there is no right answer. It is the one that you believe in and are ready to explain. Yet there is a right approach – the approach of doing your homework, understanding your business, its people, the market, the stats and the facts. Above all, the approach must be authentic.

A leader's courage to admit errors or stand by what they believe, in the face of adversity, has a secondary impact. It has a direct bearing on how they manage their people and the culture they instil. Strong leaders generally demonstrate higher levels of trust and have higher tolerance of errors, allowing a culture of confidence and positivity.

'The ultimate compelling driver to do the right thing is that someone has placed their trust in you.'

Stephen Covey

17. Holding on to trust

Since the crisis, rebuilding trust in the financial services seems to be high on several agendas. Senator Bernie Sanders included in his targets the greedy and dishonest bankers as he contested the democratic presidential nomination, taking on Hillary Clinton for the 2016 elections. Such wide spread generalisation could have unintended consequences being construed as that 'all people' in financial services are not trustworthy.

Realising that lacking trust is not good for us

In 2012, the financial services industry accounted for around 8% of UK GDP and 12% of tax receipts; financial services and related professional services employed about 7% of the working population — about 2 million people in all.[xviii] That is roughly one in 14 people in the UK. It is bad news for any economy, or society for that matter, when a population of this size and significance operates from a position of fear and lack of trust. It just does not make sense, socially, morally, ethically or economically, whichever way you look at it.

According to Brené Brown, author of *Daring Greatly*, labelling a problem in a way that makes it about who people are rather than the choices they are making lets people off the hook. She quotes from Harry Potter when Sirius told Harry to listen to him very carefully and then said, 'You're not a bad person. You're a very good person who bad things have happened to. Besides, the world isn't split into good people and Death Eaters. We've all got both light and dark inside us. What matters is the part we choose to act on. That's who we really are.' The Nine Eleven attacks in the US were a huge shock to mankind and recovery was slow and painful. The main difference between that and the banking crisis is one of attitudes; the first being a story of victims evoking empathy while this was all about criminals evoking blame and penalisation – it is this attitude that we need to change. Whether we are customers, managers or regulators, we need to learn to operate from a position of trust because not everyone in this story is a criminal, and therein lies the strength required to make a speedy recovery. Isolation is simply not a solution – if it is an option at all.

Driving improvements through trust

We need to ask ourselves, what do we want? As members of society, do we want to seek revenge or move towards a better tomorrow where people do the right thing? As leaders of firms, do we want a positive and innovative workforce or will it suffice just to have some examples that can help to demonstrate good behaviour while the rest of the organisation lives in distrust?

There are multiple ways to show good behaviour. It can be argued that the simplest and fastest way to do this may be through instilling a deep sense of fear and introducing more controls. Depending on how success is defined, this method could give us faster results. If, for example, we use reduced failure rates to measure the positive change, it may be great to see an 80% drop in failures – say a drop from 50 to 10 in any given period. We may get the results we want but not realise that in focusing efforts on telling people to make no mistakes, we might have actually signalled to them that it was just not worth trying anything new anymore. People may come to learn that sticking their head above the parapet is just too risky and that it is in their interest to plod along and carry on with their day-to-day lives. I too wonder if my book is a risky venture and if anything will come of the many hours I invest in it; will it be published, read, understood in the right spirit, and will anything change? I wonder if it might be a safer alternative to be less opinionated. I wonder if fiction may have been a safer genre for me. Only time can tell. For now, I choose to accept this risk.

There will always be reasons to fear, and reasons why it is difficult to let go and trust people. But the best way to get people do the right thing is to ensure that they want to do the right thing for the right reasons, and not out of fear. Behaviour may take more time to change, and that is okay. When change happens inside out and bottom up; it is a force to be reckoned with.

Jonathan Livingston Seagull, by Richard Bach, carries the power it does, only because Jonathan wanted to fly – not out of fear but out of the passion to do more and be more.

Weeding out fear

While fear may give you some improved metrics, it will have an adverse impact on other metrics such as the rate of innovation, creativity, and speed of change; a blame culture cause attrition, though the fall-out may not be evident for a while – even if organisations see numbers that should give rise to concern, given the silos in which several organisations operate, it may take a while to draw correlations.

If, as leaders, we continue to demonstrate low levels of trust and combine that with reduced tolerance for errors and a high level of checks, over time individuals will become less passionate, playing by the rules in a way that organisational goals will morph into annual objectives, but there won't be any dreams worth aspiring to. We may see signs such as individuals not wanting to take responsibility for their actions; wanting to push decisions anyone else, be it a committee or a manager, and if ever they are under fire, people will look for someone to blame. These are signs of a culture where fear subsumes trust so that it is not okay to make a mistake because you are being watched and a single mistake may mean loss of face and even more checks to live with.

What we want is a set of people working to achieve something meaningful. Leaders can create this ethos by trusting people to do just that. More than ever before, we need individuals to feel empowered, working to deliver to a common purpose with confidence and self-belief as opposed to a clusters of disengaged employees, immersed in fear, confusion, self-doubt and frustration.

Seeing sense in embracing trust

I understand that with past examples showing people in powerful positions breaching trust, it may be natural to enter into any conversation with a position of distrust; but while trusting people is a risk, not trusting people is, in my view, the greater risk – a risk we can ill afford. In 2015, as the bullish markets appeared to be ageing, countries seem to be faced with challenges to raise productivity and aim for business optimisation. There is a need to streamline processes and this pressure for increased investor returns will continue.

As Richard Rierson discusses in *The Speed of Trust*, his podcast with Stephen Covey, at a time like this, it is inefficient for firms to fall into this cultural trap of distrust where there are people checking people checking people.[xix] Organisations may gain a sense of comfort from the number of checks, only to find that people feel burnt out by the absence of trust and show less engagement, so that attrition levels are high and processes remain inefficient.

When we trust people, we can move with speed and efficiency. Trust can help this industry weed out its inefficiencies and bureaucracy because when we trust people and people trust us back, we minimise reactions and maximise the possibilities.

A research study conducted by Corporate Executive Board Company (CEB), a best-practice insight and technology company, highlighted organisational effectiveness as a key risk for 2015, stating that the percentage of people who display agile behaviours outside of the workplace is greater than those who display similar behaviours at work. It all boils down to feeling trusted.

If is often said that if you can't measure it, it doesn't

exist. When it comes to trust and distrust, if you can feel it, it exists. Even if only in your mind for that moment, it does exist and more importantly, it leaves its mark. To prove my point, I'd like you to ask yourself which you can recall more easily – instances of powerful stats or instances where someone failed to trust you? Low trust is a huge morale-killer.

Learning how to trust

As Covey points out, the quickest way to make someone trustworthy is to trust them. The quickest way to make someone untrustworthy is to show distrust. We need to call out the accountability but at the same time tell people that we trust them.

Highlighting the concept of 'smart trust' also called 'deserved trust' by Buffet, Covey says that it all begins with a high propensity to trust moving on to assessing three vital variables: the situation, the risk involved and the credibility of the people involved. The main focus is to hire people, train them right and assign clear roles before entrusting them with clear and high accountability.

Both trust and distrust are contagious. As we saw in the previous chapter, leaders should inspire trust by their actions in a way that people don't want to let them down, but they in turn must learn to extend the same trust to their teams. It's a skill that transforms managers to leaders without which we are left with too many managers, even more checkers, more and more lines of defence and not enough doers. When someone gives you a lot of trust, we don't want to let them down.

As managers, it would be wrong to decide not to trust anyone only because there may be some who may not live up to that trust. Trusting people takes courage particularly because it comes with a risk while it appears easier just to put checks in place – as we said earlier, people checking people, checking people, checking people. The many lines of defence and the many committees seem to be examples of this culture that Covey may be referring to. It's all common sense, but common sense is not always common practice.

If smart trust can be common practice, and we start out with the position to trust, we may discover unseen possibilities. We don't need remove all barriers in one go, but begin with trust allowing people to live up and gradually allow that atmosphere to be created. We will see some examples in the next chapter of how we can extend trust to rebuild confidence both within and outside an organisation.

'If every trade has to be a winner, your career as a trader is going to be very short.'

Lex van Dam

18. Building confidence

Imagine this.

You wake up and go to work knowing that that you are a senior manager in the city. If you make a poor decision, or if someone with the right authority deems your decision to be poor, this can culminate into a criminal offence. You and your team can cause significant harm to your firm and its customers. The bad behaviour and excessive risk taking by your peers has made headlines in the past and continues to do so. Customers expect to see change and regulators spend significant time and energy in developing new regulation to enforce the change they wish to see. You have multiple objectives which include pressing on with your day job to run the business and return shareholder value, implementing a culture change to prove that your organisation has improved its behaviours and spending time cleaning up past issues that surface from time to time. You can see housekeeping issues that need to be fixed, but those might have to wait because the change agenda is already very heavy.

You feel like you are running a car, which is creaking for attention. You need to get it serviced or even just refuel it, but you must just keep driving because stopping is not an option.

How exciting – and then we wonder why employee morale is low while attrition and customer complaints remain high.

Recognising the need for confidence

As we've seen in the previous chapter, the industry today needs change that instils confidence and not erodes it. Confidence in people who serve customers and confidence in customers being served by the banks. Changes such as pricing simplification strategies and the drive for clearer communications seem to have addressed this to some extent but more needs to be done. The need for more regulatory reporting, more evidence, more checks, more regulation and more controls may have its place but does very little to build confidence.

Providing frameworks and not approvals

Once leaders decide to extend trust and rebuild confidence, they need to find creative and effective ways to do this. They need to stop providing approvals focusing instead on ways to equip and empower customers and teams with the ability to make their own decisions.

Lex van Dam is a London-based hedge fund manager who conceived and featured in the three-part series, *Million Dollar Traders* on BBC2 in 2009. At his Lex van Dam Trading Academy, he uses the trading psychology model that is employed to assess mental toughness or strength. Although he uses the model in a trading context, I feel it has universal application because at the core, it refers to the psychology required to make tough and timely decisions in the face of constantly changing variables.

The five factors are:

1. Motivation – Why you are trading? In our context why are you in business?
2. Self-confidence – Do you believe in your ability?
3. Focus – Are you distracted and prone to mistakes?
4. Composure – How do you behave under pressure?
5. Resilience – Can you keep getting up after setbacks?

These are very personal traits, but what leaders need is for their teams to be able to develop toughness of this level, being able to demonstrate it repeatedly and consistently, in success and in failure. We really don't need more phenomenal people, nor do we need more checkers and auditors, and we definitely don't need more committees. All we need is for more ordinary people to do something a little less ordinary by demonstrating more grit and confidence to make decisions and for leaders to learn to trust them as they make these decisions.

Allowing room for mistakes

As we clamp down on our tolerance for poor conduct, employees appear to be moving from being risk aware to becoming risk averse. At one of my panel discussions, one risk manager said that he no longer cared about doing the right thing; the only thing he cared about was to make sure he did nothing wrong. His mantra was take no chances – when in doubt, just keep out of it.

Perhaps we could try that – never to take a risk and never to make a change. But wouldn't that drive complaints and dissatisfaction too, because our customers might feel that we just couldn't keep up with changing times? So what do we do? The surest way to guarantee zero detriment and zero dissatisfaction is to have no customers.

We have to allow room for mistakes. If more and more risk managers develop a stance of taking no chances, making change is going to become even more slow and frustrating. In running an organisation and managing risk, it's not so much about the decisions as it is about the process that people undergo in arriving at the decision, their understanding of the underlying story and finally, their rationale.

Imagine if, in the case of internet safety, when rating 100 sites as inappropriate for children, we allowed ourselves to be ruled by the fear that we might have missed one or two and dragged our heels with the approval process because we didn't want to be accountable for any unintentional omission or oversight. That would be a shame. Once, when discussing the potential fallout of a risky change, Pete Horrell, the ex–CEO for Barclays Wealth, explained to me that we need to weigh the risk of doing something against the risk of doing nothing. He explained that the risk of standing still could be greater than the risk of making a change.

In the same vein, Van Dam adds that 'In trading, people have a chance of actually making money, and when they lose money, they have a chance to learn something about themselves.' That is exactly the culture we should aim to drive. A culture where people have a chance to think, and be their own individuals and develop their style as opposed to one where they feel reluctant to take any action without someone else's approval. As in the cake shop analogy, there can be many ways to analyse the same situation and multiple answers to identical scenarios. There are seldom any right or wrong answers and we need to strengthen the pipeline to be able to be able to do the analysis and make the decision.

Leaders need to send out messages to their teams that it's okay to make mistakes as long as they are not culpable, wilful, criminal or blatantly irresponsible acts driven by the motivation to cause harm. Risk in itself is not bad, but we need to have the right way to take risks, accepting that decisions will be specific to context and reflective of individuals' leadership styles.

While I love the proactive mindset, the good conduct management requires, I sometimes feel that its implementation is somewhat restrained, reactive and dated. To apply such a forward-looking concept in an archaic fashion would limit the potential that the concept could offer. It would be a bit like releasing the most modern soundtracks with quality music on old style tape cassettes or watching a 4D film on a 2D TV. To get conduct management right, we need to overhaul, or at least broaden, our approach to risk to make it less regimental and more tolerant so it can keep up with conduct. Look at it this way – if conduct management is about proactive decisions, horizon scans and potential harm, how can anyone always be right without boiling the ocean? It's no surprise I get questions like, what if the building were to collapse – is that a conduct risk? We need to accept that people don't have a crystal ball, yet decisions need to be made; and while a majority may be right, some lessons may need to be learnt the hard way.

As for Horrell's point, while the fallout of a decision may be open to scrutiny, in making that decision, the disaster that was averted will remain unseen.

Decoding it for customers

Understanding finance can be overwhelming and much of the crisis can be attributed to the fact that it was just too complex for people to understand. Adding more layers of complexity will make it harder to decode and prone to further exploitation. We need to focus energies on simplifying the system and educating customers up to a point where they can understand their options and decide what is best for them, inspiring confidence as we do so.

Let's take a look at a refreshingly positive effort along these lines. In the series mentioned above, Lex van Dam set out to educate eight ordinary people about the stock market, putting a sterling equivalent of $1 million of his money for the novices to trade with over the course of eight weeks. He set up the experiment to encourage the public to take greater control of their personal finances in the wake of the financial crisis.

The only skills he was looking for was the ability to handle stress and demonstrate good math skills. Interestingly, he covered ethics in the interviews, asking people if they would you screw someone over to get ahead. Answers ranged from 'No, never' to 'I wouldn't like to, but if I had to I would.'

As the show unfolded, the British Chamber of Commerce said that the economy faced a serious risk of recession and there were fresh concerns about the health of banks around the world. The credit crisis loomed as the participants' training came to an end. Skills they learnt included self-control, desire and determination, and they were there to check whether it was possible to trade ethically and still make money.

Adding to the credibility of the show, Van Dam put his own money on the line saying, 'The million dollars for me is very significant and I can't afford to lose it. If I lose the money that would be a disaster, if I lose half the money, it would be half a disaster, which is still a disaster, losing 5%, it's humiliation, and losing anything at all is terrible.'

The show got more interesting as the ground rules were laid out, and it was made clear that the idea was to ensure that people traded their own opinions with the rule being to ensure that people appreciate the risk.

That's exactly what we need more of – personally invested leaders who care enough to select the right people, train them, define the rules and then step back, allowing people to get on with it. We all know that a tremendous desire to control all decisions is damaging. Perhaps it's no surprise when you hear that John McFarlane, the CEO of Barclays, cringed at the bureaucracy in his organisation, saying that Barclays had '375 management committees – and that is 370-something too many. This is about trying to work it with zero.'[xx] The issue is not limited to Barclays and, if anything, I would applaud the bank for acknowledging and seeking to address this over-complexity.

Helping customers decide

Barclays Local Insights is a good example of putting control back in customers' hands by helping them decide. How this works is that Barclays uses aggregated and anonymised client data already available to the bank to provide useful insights about people and small businesses in local communities. The tool is available to everyone and is not restricted to Barclays customers.[xxi]

The site is easy to use and all it does is give you information such as customer spending in your area by industry, age and income bands. I like this example because it makes creative use of data giving power back to people by saying, 'Here's what we know – you decide' without compromising anyone's personal information.

The end objective is to help people make better decisions. Isn't that what good conduct is all about?

Barclays SmartSpend is similar example which provides customers with a comparison tool enabling them to input information such as gender and age to view the average spend of people like them. For example, I can see that on average people in the same category as me have spent an average of £43 on water bills and £105 on council tax bills. The site could also be used to compare and switch energy providers, digital providers etc.

Looking at a service such as this from a customer's viewpoint, it enables them to make more informed decisions at no added cost to them and is a good example of doing things right by customers. These are also examples of how conduct can improve customer experience. In chapter 20, we will explore this relationship between conduct and customer experience.

Get the controls right

Once firms establish the principles for conduct, they need to check their existing frameworks, policies and controls to determine what enhancements are needed.

Speaking of controls, I have a vivid recollection of my granddad's home in India (Indore) where we went for all our summer breaks. It was a lovely three-story family home with many doors, windows and large balconies where we played carom for hours. The odd thing was that with each visit, we noticed more metal grills at the windows, more locks in the doors, the balconies were sealed and the security just kept getting tighter until the beautiful family home started to feel like a mini fortress.

We asked our grandmother what was going on. She blamed my granddad and said that that each time he heard of another robbery in the city, he brought in the locksmith to secure the house a little more. I am sure that in his eternal wisdom, he felt compelled to do more to protect his family. In similar vein, risks managers often describe their role as one to 'protect the firm'. We will come back to that thought.

Building confidence is paramount to today's financial scenario. This confidence is not limited to regulators or the market's confidence in banks but it includes customers' and banks' confidence in themselves. We need systems that meet our requirements, and we need to build in controls that are proportionate to the risk, but at the heart of it all, we need people who feel confident enough to operate these systems at their full potential as we learn to take a step back and allow people to get on with what we have tasked them to do.

'This idea is simple but fundamental: banks stop making money from encouraging customers to spend theirs on things they might not need, and start profiting from helping them to save money on the things they really do. It sounds obvious. It could be the future of banking. The race is on.'

Gillian Guy

19. Establishing the right culture

Conduct and culture are very closely linked in that culture has a direct impact on the way an organisation conducts itself. We have seen in previous examples that this is true not only of organisations but of families, nations, religions and many other ways that people come together to form a unit.

Edward T. Hall suggested that culture was like an iceberg with behaviour being the tip that is visible to the eye. The rest of the iceberg was made up of beliefs, attitudes and, at its core, values.

Since behaviours on display are only that tip of that iceberg, changing behaviour is relatively easy in comparison to changing culture – because the change would merely be a superficial one. It would also be short-lived because core values remain unchanged. Hence when looking to remediate behaviour, we must be sensitive to values and make that our starting point.

To change the culture of an organisation is so easy and yet so difficult. Easy because it doesn't require large amounts of IT infrastructure or many hours of training. Difficult because training efforts, emails, town halls and other internal updates can only do so much to help impart information regarding the desired culture; making a genuine cultural shift requires regular nurturing and leadership by example.

There are two types of culture in any organisation. The first is the espoused culture, which is normally promoted through established organisational channels – the one that you see on websites and brochures; and then there is the real culture which people live and breathe. It is this culture that you witness in intense meetings, at the smoking zones and in performance conversations.

As organisations try to bring their real culture close to the espoused ones, attempts to regulate behaviour may exhibit disconnect if organisational values are not aligned with expected behaviours. Simply put, people may note that we don't practise as we preach – the cultural iceberg will show cracks.

While culture is a topic too vast to cover in this book,

I have listed some ideas to explore when addressing conduct as part of the overall culture.

Being authentic

An authentic leader is great culture personified. An organisation's cultural journey is determined by what the leader says and does. If leaders are lacking in authenticity, efforts to drive a cultural change could be pointless.

In the conduct context, this authenticity comes from how leaders conduct themselves and way they handle various dilemmas related to conduct. This includes various finer points such as the leader's notion of conduct, their attitude towards teams and customers, their willingness to listen, their thought process, their problem-solving skills and their ability to make the really tough decisions and be transparent about it.

Whether leadership has a vested interest in the future of the organisation or is filled with short-term thinking lacking a connection to an organisation's future, it will have a bearing on the culture. While studies suggest that the average tenure of CEOs has decreased in the past years, the tenure itself is not a worry; it is more about the commitment and attitude displayed. Leaders need to ask themselves if they are really showing genuine commitment themselves or lurking on the periphery doing just enough to ensure that they are seen to do the right things. Do they really care? What methods do they use to communicate that they are invested?

Besides appointed leaders, organisations have culture carriers. These people may not have a formal leadership role, but carry a huge about of influence on people – albeit informally. In the context of culture, culture carriers need to be seen as leaders too.

Learning from family companies

In a very interesting podcast from *The Economist,*[xxiii] Adrian Woolridge explores family companies. Family companies are companies owned and run by families, or owned by families but run by management (Walmart), or may be regarded as the family run where families have a small number of shares, such as Toyota and Samsung.

In the conduct context, what sets them apart from other non-family run businesses is long-termism; the fact that that they have a view to the future. Not because of a fear of fines, but out of a deep connection with the brand. Such companies tend to continue to thrive in emerging economies: there are large set-ups of family run business in places like Hong Kong, India, Philippines, and China. Woolridge quoted Berry Brothers, a London-based wine company founded in 1698, which has been running for seven generations with its motto being that it is built to last. The company is run from the same premises in St James's in London where it first opened its doors in 1698. Public companies, in contrast, are more prone to be prey to short-term managers and short-term owners who may prioritise share value in comparison to a long-term brand value.

I'm not suggesting that one is better than the other, as family companies come with their own downsides – 60% of Asian companies lost value when the patriarch died. All I am saying is that there is something to be learnt from them.

However, even in these cases, there may be exceptions. Heather Cho, daughter of the owner of Korean air, a family-run company, forced a plane to return to the gate in New York and offload a steward because she did not like the way she had been served nuts.[xxiv] Legacy and power bring great responsibility to ensure good conduct, and yet there are exceptions now and again.

Other examples of differently run organisations include the John Lewis Partnership, where employees have a stake and employees are partners. I once met a Waitrose employee over a family gathering. He buzzed about how he always arrived early for work because it was his business and he was an owner; he was easily one of the most motivated employees I have ever met. Waitrose is operated by the John Lewis Partnership.

Overall, while businesses will continue to have different structures, more could be done to deepen this connection between employees and the firm so that employees associate the firm's conduct and reputation with their own.

Recognising the other icebergs floating about

While we acknowledge that behaviour is only the tip of the cultural iceberg and find ways to institutionalise core behaviours as part of the belief system of an organisation, we need to accept that organisations do not and should not exist in isolation.

While we can control our own recruitment policies and guard our values, we need to acknowledge that as we live in a global world, and influence other organisations as we are influenced by them. Just as strong as the need to protect our culture is the need to understand the culture of those around us, and therefore organisations must operate from a position of strength as opposed to fear, because in fear there is weakness, and that is when we give in to temptation.

Therefore to get cultures right, besides getting the right type of people and training them well, leaders need to do more to inculcate a deep sense of belonging that gives people the power to stand strong in the face of temptation or poor examples in the external world.

Often I am asked how I allow my children to spend time on the internet and if that would be poor influence. Sooner or later they will be exposed to this world – the great and the ghastly. I would rather that they experience it bit by bit while I am around for them to ask questions and check their beliefs, rather than protecting them too much, leaving them potentially more vulnerable to what they may experience without my support.

Taking reactions through to results

The one common problem with communication is we often assume that if something has been communicated, it has been understood and applied, and applied correctly. I cannot stress enough on this point especially in the context of change in global organisations particularly when it relates to something as intangible as conduct. I'll use the Kirkpatrick model to demonstrate my point. Explaining levels of learning, this model is a really useful way to assess if messages have resulted in outcomes.

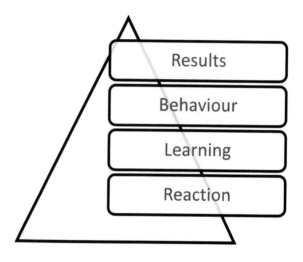

Figure 6: Levels of Learning

According to the model, there are four levels of learning:

1. Reaction: This is the first level, when I attend a training session or course and come away with an initial reaction such as that I think the session was useful. This is often assessed through participant feedback surveys (also called reaction sheets).
2. Learning: This is the second level, where I need to be able to prove that I have acquired some knowledge, skills or attitudes as a result of that session. This is usually assessed through course evaluations, including pre- and post-course evaluations.

3. Behaviour: This is the third level, where I start to put that learning into practice and there is a difference in my behaviour as I apply the learning when doing the job. This can be assessed by change in performance or peer feedback, e.g. if I were to be trained on conduct, there might be an expectation to see a reduction of incidents related to poor conduct.

4. Results: At this fourth level, we hope to see results because the outcomes that we intended to achieve through the training should have been achieved. Continuing with the example of conduct, by this stage you may expect that an organisation enjoys more customer trust, e.g. more customers recommending us to friends, potentially even reduced fines and penalties.

I understand that it may be difficult for companies to apply that level of rigour to any change, but we must not kid ourselves that communication would directly result in cultural change; there is much to be verified.

A simpler way to try and confirm cultural change may by taking a 'slice', as Malcolm Gladwell puts in his book *Blink*. While it is not as thorough as the Kirkpatrick model, it offers some form of verification and enables people to flag key gaps. Organisations often use this in the form of employee surveys, pulse check or other similarly named actions.

Regardless of how we confirm that cultural change is not a myth, it is important that we do so. When communicating, we would do well to ask ourselves if we are communicating for communication sake or if we really care to be understood. Assuming we were understood what is the change we wish to see? How will we verify the change?

Leaders must be articulate about the change they wish to see explaining clearly that if culture and conduct were really well embedded, what would change? Would they have more information or the same amount of information with better results, would the organisation be talking conduct all the time, or would they stop talking about conduct and be speaking of customers instead? When leaders are unable to articulate what they expect to see, or are not aligned in these expectations, there is likely to be confusion and wastage.

There may be a change I expect to see

The perfect change that will set us free...

But unless I cannot define that change –

At best I'll sound inspirational, at worst, strange.

20. Conduct and customer experience

Let's begin with a story.

I was out with my family visiting a theme park. I stopped to pick up some food and as I collected my tray, full of doughnuts and ice creams, I bumped into one of the park employees and dropped the tray. The staff apologised and not only did he replace the entire order, he also gave us some extra spend vouchers as a gesture of goodwill.

The question here is if this good conduct or is this good customer experience? I ask because I am often asked. The two are so close together that they are often confused with one another. It may be worth taking a moment to distinguish between the two.

Here is another story, this time a true one. I was shopping at Westfield in Stratford, London, and stopped at a coffee shop. While I was deciding what I wanted, a friendly employee said, 'You look a little tired, why don't I get you a coffee from us while you decide what you'd like to have?' I was totally surprised, the gesture lifting my energy even before I had the coffee. Such acts of niceness with no underlying motive are rare. While these may be amazing examples of customer delight, I think we should take a moment to differentiate between conduct and customer experience.

I've created this diagram to help explain my point.

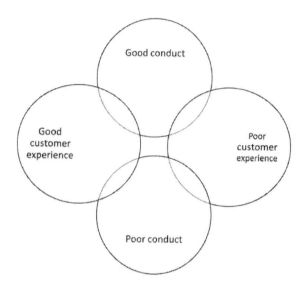

Figure 7: Conduct and Customer Experience

Good conduct means that we have done something that is right by customers or the market – customers may or may not realise it and you there is a chance that they might not like it.

Good conduct and good customer experience:

The examples from the coffee shop and the theme park were those of good conduct combined with good customer experience.

Good conduct and poor customer experience:

When sales persons refuse to serve alcohol or cigarettes to underage customers, the customers might not like it but the decision is right by them.

Good conduct and no impact on customer experience:

When organisations spend energy and time investing in back-end functions like automation, data privacy measures to keep our data secure, customers might be more secure (therefore what has been done is right by them) but they may know anything about the work that has been done, I have therefore said that there is no visible impact on customer experience.

The above three are also true of true of poor conduct. It may drive a poor client experience, a happy one or none at all because customer may not even realise that they have been through a detriment. Examples below:

Poor conduct and good customer experience:

In the PPI scenario, the initial customer experience might have been a good one because customers who paid for the product may have felt a certain peace of mind having insured themselves. The fact that the product didn't really serve good outcomes was unknown to them at the outset. The horsemeat scandal is similar because people might have left supermarkets with a good experience believing that they had bought a product they wanted.

Poor conduct and poor customer experience:

The same examples of PPI and the horsemeat scandal became cases of poor customer experience once issues came to light. Other examples may be that customers are sent unclear or misleading communications.

Poor conduct and no impact on customer experience:

This could relate to the many historic issues that banks are trying to remediate where customers may not know that they have been through some harm, e.g. incorrect interest rates being applied or system outages that customers didn't notice.

In a nutshell, not all good experience leads to good outcome and not all bad experience has bad outcome. The two may constantly converge and diverge but are fundamentally different disciplines.

'Data is like water. The world is covered in it. But only 3 percent is usable.'

Anonymous

21. Understanding data and metrics

Information is power. Leaders are exposed to significant amounts of information every day, but conduct is about information, combined with insight and intuition. Leaders needs to ask themselves what information they need, what is it telling them and what they need to do about the information presented to them?

We are all aware that there is just too much information out there and it is only expected to grow exponentially. Which is precisely why we need to be able to seek carefully. While gathering and understanding information may require scientific expertise and skill, putting it to effective use in the conduct context is more of an art.

There is significant industry level discussion and debate about what the key conduct MI should include.

Defining metrics

Firms need to be clear on what they are measuring

and what they are not. In this desire to measure everything, metrics can often be poorly defined, so they actually tell you very little. Even worse, they could give you a misleading picture.

Imagine a metric such as number of complaints responded to within two weeks. At first, it might sound all right if a report were to say that we responded to all complaints in two weeks' time. On scratching below the surface, we may find that 'respond' means that we had sent an initial response acknowledging receipt with a message saying, 'We have received your complaint and someone from the team will contact you in two to four weeks.' It might actually mean that customers could be expected to wait up to six weeks before someone actually responded to them.

Metrics should not therefore be taken at face value – we need to query what they are telling us. Let's look at how this works with car dashboards. A *Daily Mail* article[xxv] reported research revealing that Britain's motorists were becoming a nation of 'dashboard dunces' and were baffled by the increasing array of warning lights in their cars. More than nine in ten people failed to recognise one particular warning. The study identified 99 separate dashboard light warnings in 15 of the UK's most popular cars ranging from a Nissan hatchback to Mercedes-Benz executive saloons. Just 12 of the symbol designs were common across all models. Ninety five percent people couldn't identify the faulty catalytic converter.

Take a moment and ask yourself if you would be able to identify the faulty catalytic converter or its equivalent in your organisation. Would you be able to spot the issues of the future – the PPIs of tomorrow?

Looking at it from all aspects

When speaking of stocks, Van Dam says, 'you need to have an idea of fundamental value... if you don't have an idea or opinion on the value of something, then how can you know if it's cheap or it's expensive?'[xxvi] In the context of trading, he says that each time you look at a stock from various aspects, you're going to know a lot. You need to have a good idea and you want to know that the idea is backed up.

Metrics are the same. You need to know what you are looking at and determine what you are looking for, and then look at it from all aspects. As we showed in the case of trust, you need to be able to join the dots, draw the connection and the correlations that are not always so obvious. For that, it is imperative to understand your business and have a genuine stake. For that reason, I draw examples from trading, because it's one of the places you see real stake where people put their money where their mouth is. The other is our children. In both scenarios, we are fully invested.

Figures on their own are meaningless and need to be seen in relation to something – in the context of everything else that is going on. When stocks and currencies were being hammered in August 2015, you had to have an understanding of the thread tangled through everything – whether it was the China slowing down, Russia dealing with falling oil prices, the Fed contemplating interest rates, Brazil with corruption or Turkey with its political instability. Similarly if organisations feel that the their change agenda is large, failures have increased, customer satisfaction is low, employee attrition is high, leaders need to be able to find that thread, the pulse so they can address the cause and avoid treating symptoms in isolation. Conducting an organisation well is about this ability to be able to find this thread, and deciding what needs done in given circumstances. It is also about knowing if the dashboard is missing essential pieces of information and asking for them to be made available.

The burning question: are we there yet?

One of the unintended fallouts of fixing it all here and

now is analysis paralysis, also called paralysis by analyses – a state in which we overthink things, often to the point where we make no decision and take no meaningful action.

One cue would be when reports tell us the same things from one period to another, almost to the point where we can't tell one report from the next. To me, that is a warning sign that we are measuring too often, fixing too little, or maybe we just have the wrong metrics. Or we are so far removed from the process that we just can't tell the difference – words and numbers are just a blur.

Repeated measurement distracts people working on a fix and can also impact employee morale because when effort spent in reporting is misaligned to the pace of change, people can feel burnt out reporting the same content over and over, possibly concluding that all reporting goes into a black hole, and conversations suggest that none of this is ever read.

For those who need figures at their fingertips, automation could be worthwhile. I can't imagine Twitter having to run a report each time I wanted to know how many followers I have. The information is real time and always readily available and because it is so intuitively designed, we even know where to find it.

While the added focus may be a by-product of the tightening regime, and the fear of failure or even a symptom of a situation where people just want to cover themselves, we need to accept that if asking the same questions more often meant that we get there sooner, we may do well to check our bank accounts every hour.

Identifying if you need conduct MI

So what is conduct MI? If every decision can be linked to conduct, and every failure can hurt customers, then isn't every metric a conduct metric?

The short answer is yes, if you truly get conduct, your business MI should be your conduct MI, because your day-to-day metrics will be broad and well-rounded ensuring that conduct issues come to surface as you run the business. It's like driving a car.

You need to do your five point checks before you set off – this is like the absolute minimum you would confirm before you start something new such as to launch a new product, new service or enter a new market.

Once you begin to drive, your dashboard tells you about your speed, fuel consumption etc. In business this is your business-as-usual MI; the information you use on an ongoing basis.

And then there are the 13 hazard types you constantly watch for e.g. children and the elderly, emerging vehicles, vehicles turning left or right. These are external factors like key emerging risks, regulatory focus etc. We need to keep looking out for these.

Just as we conduct ourselves responsibly when driving a car, conduct needs to be infused in the entire journey of running an organisation – starting from the point where we define our strategy to the point where we check why customers are leaving us. We don't drive carefully because there is a risk that we will conduct ourselves poorly, we drive carefully because that's what you do. Are any of the metrics related to driving about conduct? Not really. They are about driving responsibly and making sure you have all the information you need to be able to do so. Good conduct is therefore the outcome.

Recognising that faulty catalytic converter

People often wonder how much MI is enough and I often here discussions around the magic number of conduct metrics for any given organisation – should this be the top three or the top 20?

I would say that it's a wasted debate. Imagine it as if you were on iTunes – you should be able to have any cut you like. Just as you can filter your music by genre, new music, recent releases, songs, albums, videos, or just run a simple search your MI should give you the same flexibility as you may wish to slice information to find your patterns.

When it comes to numbers, one size doesn't fit all. Going back to the car analogy, models vary from the Volvo S40 and Nissan Micra with 20 odd messages to the Mercedez-Benz E Class that has over 40 messages. Then there is the Audi A3 with 28. You have a choice to determine what want you want to be able to see so you can make informed decisions about your business – just remember that more important than searching for Conduct MI is the business MI, which tells you about how the business is being conducted – and this MI should include conduct metrics. While there is no magic number to this dashboard, it's good to have a cross section that follows the business journey and gives you an insight into each area. Here below are some questions that you should want your MI to be able to answer.

Product: How does the product creation work? Does it have robust governance? If so, is it being followed as intended? Are the products meeting customers' needs? Are customers using these products? Are they complaining about the products? Could it be that they have some products that are not good for them?

Technology: How stable and resilient is your technology? What is your outage data? Do your customers get the right reports at the right time? How do you generate, store and safeguard customer data (even when outsourced)? Is customers' data safe with you? How do you gain comfort that you protect your systems from failure and attack? Do you manipulate this data in more intelligent ways to generate adequate MI to inform sales, marketing, product design and customers?

People: Do people feel like they have a voice and can raise issues? Are they raising issues? Do they feel engaged enough to care? Is good behaviour identified and adequately rewarded? Is bad behaviour identified and addressed?

Horizon: You also need to have a view on the horizon which may be the new regulation coming in, interest rate changes, ring fencing requirements, election results, sanctions etc.

Emerging risks: According to a survey conducted by CEB[xxvii] in 2015, the top four emerging risks are large scale cyber-attacks, talent retention, organisational effectiveness and data control. Large scale cyber-attacks and data control might remain a large threat for a while, e.g. in the case of the attack on TalkTalk Telecom Group plc in October 2015, the Group issued a warning that customers' personal details may have been stolen. The risks and issues will change from time to time and leaders should at least have an idea of what's coming. Some regulatory focus areas include technological developments, complex terms and conditions, suitability, poor culture and controls, conflicts of interest amongst others. Organisations will of course have their own concerns to add to the generic list.

Keeping it relevant

Whatever your personal style, when it comes to conduct, I believe that there is no such thing as a static dashboard – hence it's an art. Given that conduct is about proactivity and horizons, you will want to view different things at different points in time and you need to know where to look. If you are driving in the rain, you watch for the puddles, but when it snows, you keep an eye on the tyres. And if you're driving in India, you're going to need that horn to survive.

More about problem finding than problem solving

Conduct is about problem finding as much as about problem solving. All our lives we are trained to solve problems, perhaps if we got better trained to find and acknowledge problems, we may have more emerging problems that we catch on the front foot, as opposed to a few big gaping holes that could lead to regulatory action.

It never fails to amaze me just how we learn to put up with little gremlins that creep into the system and while they take away a small percentage of our efficiency and joy each day, they rarely ever become the one big thing that scream for attention – a bit like a migraine that we learn to live with or that toothache that comes and goes.

I understand that there are finite resources and that we can only fix a few things at a time, but sometimes these solutions are unbelievably simple, we just don't care to explore. I liken that to the express checkout tills in super markets where smaller baskets should be identified and allowed to whiz through without having to queue up behind the loaded trollies.

Your metrics are driving behaviours

Measuring the wrong thing can drive the wrong behaviour.

A BBC report[xxviii] accused police in England and Wales of failing to carry out effective investigations into allegations of child abuse. 'Police had focused on talking burglary and car crime for many years, and success was measured by the number of offences and convictions... The inspectorate or Constabulary said that target driven culture must be driven out from policing instead protection of children must be at the core of what police do. Present system contains weaknesses and inconsistencies leaving children at the risk of harm.' The report cited that the police response in 220 of 576 cases it examined was inadequate. There were delays in gathering evidence and that children were not always listened to ... senior police said moving away from reactive policing and focusing more on child protection was necessary but would take time. The home office said that police must improve its response to child abuse and would have the resources to do it.

There is no excuse for measure the wrong thing.

'Ninety per cent of the world's data has been created in the last two years … The ultimate question is really what insight and value can we derive from that data.'

George lee

22. Conduct and Big Data

I'm often asked what conduct has to do with Big Data. Hopefully, by now you will be with me on the fact that conduct has to do with everything. Big data is basically data collected and mined at a really large scale. This is the huge amount of data we leave about ourselves as we go about our lives such as our where about, our social media interactions, our Wi-Fi usage, our purchase history etc. The key purpose of big data is for an organisation to be able to harness the data, convert it into information and use their knowledge to put the information to right use. Once data is mined, it needs to be put to use in a way that helps customers.

Oracle estimates suggest that data is growing at a 40% compound annual rate and I can reel out more stats. But stats suggest that you are more likely to remember the stories so let's do some stories instead and we can understand its link to conduct.

Using the data in the background

One way to use big data is to deliver tailor made solutions for customers based on what we know about them using algorithms or complex statistics to recommend specific options. Most dating apps use information provided by users to recommend options. With 25% of us today[xxix] finding their partners via dating apps, these apps have changed the face of traditional dating. For those of who don't know how it works, the apps generally use this increasingly granular customer data such as our location and other preferences to suggest potential dates. Every move we make creates data, which is then used all over the world to provide real time value to customers, this is just one example.

What has this to do with conduct? These are simple honest apps that use our information with consent to help provide suitable solutions. I only mention it to explain how data is being used in multiple ways and that more of us are impacted by these changes in more ways than we may care to accept. Big data and its benefits can contribute to driving and managing the cultural change needed to accommodate conduct considerations. It can help to improve how we engage with new and existing customers and need to be put to use carefully and creatively, e.g. it can inform our product development and marketing structures, our sales process, our compensation and staff motivation it can help us evidence workflows which can come in need, and must never be overlooked as a standalone piece that has nothing to do with conduct.

Combining technology to drive good outcomes

No single technology application is as transformative as the combinations, e.g. mobile phones and internet technology combined with fingerprint scan or vein scanning. Let's look at the Beacon Initiative that was trialled by Barclays in 2015 to help customers' accessibility needs within branch banking. What this essentially does is allow customers with special needs to pre-register via an App that stores a client's accessibility needs and a photo, and once the customer is in the range or the branch, the app senses the beacon and alerts branch.

This is a great example of using a beacon combined with the app, the in-branch iPads and the data that the firm holds to provide truly good outcomes. The trial was incepted as an outcome of a client complaint about the frustration of having to explain their accessibility needs repeatedly.

Recognising that technology is not the risk

People often fear that rapid technology change put

consumers and firms at risk and people sometimes try to shun technology. That is a very limited view of the world. Technology, used correctly, opens a world of possibilities. It has so much to offer to the economy, organisations and us – the people behind it all. There is risk, a lot of risk. There is the risk that systems will fail and impact a large number of customers and that the velocity with which the risk arises or the issue hits, will give us little time to respond, if any. There is also the risk that automated, intertwined processes mean that the exposure is much greater. In time, it will complicate and simplify life even further. Products such as Hive, take information from live environment, making product design more complex and dynamic. So while it's simple to you at the customer, the stuff going on behind the scenes gets more and more complicated.

When regulators fined JP Morgan's UK wealth management business for failing to keep complete and up-to-date information the issue it worth accepting that the right technology can help with evidence and prevent issues such as these. There are infinite ways to put technology to use and what is does is only limited by an organisation's creativity and appetite. The ultimate aim is to use the insights to propel the business forward, while serving client interests.

Always remember the human factor. While big data

can deliver amazing benefits by harnessing the insight, what one person finds delightful may be intrusion for another. Although it opens up a world of opportunities, Big Data can be on a collision route with consumer preferences and conduct and we need to put an extra bit of onus as we leverage the opportunities presented by big data.

23. Developing a holistic view

What is the difference between conduct and operational risk? How do you tell if something is a conduct risk or an operational risk, or both?

Questions such as these that relate to the definition and taxonomy just refuse to go away. Too many people are unclear regarding this and too much time is spent differentiating between the two. More painful is the fact that there are multiple versions of the truth that coexist.

Clarifying the taxonomy

I was invited to speak about conduct at the OpRisk 2015 conference. Hosted by Operational Risk & Regulation, this is the industry's leading conference gathering 200 plus senior operational risk directors and regulators from across the globe. Before I was called on the stage, the gentleman making my introduction added that if there was one thing he knew about conduct risk, it was that it doesn't exist. The comments were an eye opener into the debate between the two schools. Following this event, people have told me that conduct risk is a fad, just a gimmick; the regulators' desperate effort to convince customers that they were doing their bit to correct the banks' behaviours. Just too much time is being spent on classification and categorisation followed by re-classification and re-categorisation.

The same issues also result in a conflict of interest between teams that represent different types of risk. This happens naturally when conversations are centered around how best to categorise a risk as opposed to how best to mitigate the risk.

For example, India has 29 states and given the vast number of religions and languages, and when in India, I often witnessed rifts between people trying to uphold their own religion or sub-community. However, once people step out of the country, you see a remarkable shift in mindsets as we begin to see ourselves as Indians before being Delhiites or Mumbaiites and develop a sense of pride in anything Indian.

Changing mindsets

Banks badly need this change in mindset, stepping away from little universes of conduct risk and operational risk or any other risk for that matter, focusing instead on the bigger picture so we can see the risks for what they are and decide where energies are best spent Again, a very small change but one that can completely overhaul future design principles. We need to focus less on the categories and more on the role of risk management as a holistic function that looks at risks, reports them in their entirety while remaining focused on the business purpose and global developments as opposed to getting bogged down by internal categorisations.

I wonder why it is a surprise to anyone that as banks have captured more conduct risks, the count of operational risks seems to have seen a decline. If an organisation had a finite amount of risks each month and instead of logging them all under a single banner, now needs to split these amongst two categories, it would be obvious to expect a drop. Given the confused taxonomy, it would also be natural to expect that the split will be inconsistent between and within organisations, which will potentially result in incomparable data.

Here is a classic example:

The FCA fined three leading banks £42 million for IT failures that occurred in June 2012 and meant that the banks' customers could not access banking services. [xxx]

These fines were a result of the banks' failure to put in place resilient IT systems that could withstand, or minimise, the risk of IT failures. The actual cause of the IT incident was a software compatibility problem caused by the banks' failure to put in place adequate systems and controls to identify and manage their exposure to IT risks. This incident affected 6.5 million customers in the United Kingdom for several weeks. Over that time, customers could not use online banking facilities to access their accounts or obtain accurate account balances from ATMs; customers were unable to make timely mortgage payments; customers were left without cash in foreign countries; the Banks applied incorrect credit and debit interest to customers' accounts and produced inaccurate bank statements; and some organisations were unable to meet their payroll commitments or finalise their audited accounts.

The question here is whether this is a conduct risk, an operational risk, a technology risk, a change management risk or all of the above.

The more important question is if you would like to see this issue reflected in three different logs, worded in three different ways, updated three times each month, discussed at three or more committees and being addressed by three or more programmes?

Six months on, would you like to see it flagged amber on one chart and red on another while teams spend time discussing and debating how best to reconcile their ratings? Alternatively, would you rather see it on one place and everyone working in collaboration to fix things, learn lessons, and move on?

'It doesn't make sense to hire smart people and then tell them what to do; we hire smart people so they can tell us what to do.'

Steve Jobs

24. Leaving a trail

Always leave a trail. If you can't prove it happened, it didn't happen.

Let's face it, when you're focused on dealing with issues, leaving evidence is the last thing on your mind. Especially when moments are tense and the world is looking to you for decisions, you want to be trusted and supported and not asked for more and more evidence. Instant decisions are followed by quick actions and there is a certain pace about things. Quite right. At a time when we are hard pressed for agility and productivity, collecting evidence may seem cumbersome and futile.

But we need to find ways to answer how the culture has changed. Ways to explain how customers are front and centre of all decisions.

Asking the questions

The need for evidence is often driven by the regulators' desire to see conduct principles assimilated in each and every move that an organisation makes. Quoting from the FCAs second annual report, 'Every important financial decision an individual makes or that a firm is involved in, must have a clear emphasis on good conduct.'

While conduct is loosely defined, the interpretation of this requirement is even looser. Suddenly, the absence of a poor intention is not sufficient. There needs to be an explicit, demonstrable, auditable emphasis. This creates confusion, not because firms are ill intended, but because they are grappling with how to demonstrate this conduct emphasis, for how many decisions, for how long? Common questions that firms are asking include:

- How do we demonstrate good conduct?
- Will it suffice to evidence the lack of any intentional poor conduct?
- Is there a way to use technology to drive and demonstrate good conduct?
- Should we be speaking of conduct as a separate topic or should it be part of all discussions?
- What MI do we need to evidence to show that we consider conduct as part of day-to-day decisions?

Other broader questions include:

- What is the correct MI that can give senior leaders assurance that conduct is being well managed?
- Is this a temporary 'thing' or will this be business as usual?
- Do we not need a full team just to be doing this?

Asking the real questions

Questions are fundamental to learning I genuinely like and encourage them. But the state of flux combined with lacking focus on the real issues that comes though these questions is worrisome. Yes, firms have messed up, and there is certainly room for improvement but there is also room for improvement in the approach to evidencing. It may be more heartening if discussions were focused on real issues.

- What should be our strategic focus and how do we know this?
- Are we really providing value for money?
- How do we give our customers a better service?
- Where do my customers feel let down?
- What are they complaining about and how can I ensure I address key complaint reasons and aim for end-to-end improvements?

- How can my business teams and risk functions be better aligned?
- How do I create meaningful MI that gives me real time statistics when something is not working?

Being busy without being efficient

The focus on being able to produce a credible evidence pack sometimes consumes us and often we scupper around collecting evidence, seeking comfort in this false sense progress that we get from the busy-ness of things. We seem to be busy, and we are. But it's so easy to be busy and yet be inefficient.

I took a moment to reflect on what evidence may mean as a parent, if parents had to demonstrate how well they look after their children and I was told that I could have a supervisor come in to look for evidence. Maybe I would need to work through a list of the meals I had given to them, a log of activities quickly getting tedious and I might get consumed by the recording, and in doing so, be paying less attention to the children.

Beginning with the end in mind

When Covey says begin with the end in mind, he invites us to design the end vision toward which we will work. I invite you to ask of your organisation, what is it that you want to be able to prove in three to five years' time? Would it be that they produced a fantastic evidence pack or that they went about their business in such an effective way, bearing in mind clients, colleagues and markets in everything they did that they gave conduct a whole new meaning opening our minds to what good conduct looks like in practice.

Finding effective evidence in easy ways

Firms make decisions all day, every day. They therefore need to some very effective ways to be able to evidence the thinking behind these decisions. They need to find ways that enable them you to have a credible story without having to put in explicit effort in documentation – ways that allow them to have their story is written even when they are not writing.

In the film *Game Plan*, Joe Kingman was a football star who was single, carefree and popular. He was greeted with a surprise one morning when his eight-year-old daughter Peyton Kelly arrived at his doorstep and said she would be staying with her dad. Though they began to build a father-daughter relationship, Kingsman was quite new to this sort of thing and at the opening of his restaurant, he left without Peyton. He simply forgot.

He was then on the covers of tabloids and reporters made him miserable over his irresponsible conduct as a father. After futile efforts to retain his popularity, Peyton came to his rescue saying that he was new to this and trying the best he could, and that she thought that he was the best father in the world. That is what effective evidence looks like, though I'm not suggesting for a moment that it's okay to forget your child.

Happy customers are one way to make a point. But customers don't always know when they have suffered poor outcomes such as having paid too much for a product or having bought products that may have been unsuitable for them. Like the PPI scandal, it may take years for things to get unsurfaced if at all they do. Your approach to evidence should therefore include your story of everything that you do in the back-end to delivering good outcomes. You should be able to provide a credible story explaining how you keep an eye on customers, their needs, their issues, your resolution of those issues etc.

At a recent Big Data event in London, (BigDataFS 2015), I saw a demo by a company called Splunk. The demo showed a mobile company's real-time data on all mobile activations every second. You could see clearly how many customers were activated and what type of device they had for every second of the demo. You could add other parameters such as location. Using this, if I ran a mobile company, I could use this data to identify patterns and issues. For example, if the graph normally showed me 10 to 12 phones being activated per second and suddenly no new phones were activated for a few seconds, the change might suggest that customers were facing activation issues. This drop may cause the business to take some action and while it does so, you may not need to prepare separate evidence as to why you prioritised this action over others, because the same graphs that helped you detect the story might come in handy as evidence if there was a need to explain your actions.

Key decisions will naturally be documented, e.g. when determining your strategic direction, funding priorities etc. However, this should be a 90:10 split if anything in my view, where 90 - 95% of your evidence comes from the trail you leave behind and takes no added effort while 5 - 10% may be specific items that need to be recorded in the form of minutes etc.

As everyone understands their role to the goal, processes designs, systems and technology, training, governance will all work towards automation of the evidence trail because the most effective evidence is when you aren't working with the evidence in mind but leaving a trail anyway.

Process designers could use effective principles such as Poka yoke and Triz. Poka-yoke, a Japanese term, means mistake-proofing, and is focused on finding ways to improve the process as opposed to counting the mistakes. It is a change in thinking that means that we get proactive and think of an issue that may occur and find ways to prevent it, or raise alerts when it happens, possibly even bringing the system to a halt until we intervene. Simple day-to-day examples include the way you just can't insert a USB drive the wrong way round. Simple financial examples may be our customer systems where I just can't continue a conversation with a customer unless I have completed their identification through a password only known to them; remember a time when you were asked for the third and the fifth digit of your password and if you said all six digits, you had to rest the password?

Triz, on the other hand, is about creativity in the way that you transfer your own problem into an equivalent TRIZ problem and then check the TRIZ solution with the aim of applying that analogy to your solution.[xxxi]

It's like this. Most of us are godfearing people, but before we make any decision, we don't justify how the decision relates to our fear of God. We just get on with what we do and it is not until we hit a crossroad faced with dilemmas that we sit back and think about what would be the right thing to do. We need to get to that point where that day-to-day positive intent becomes an unspoken common denominator and a part of the organisational culture. While we all share the need to evidence our discussions to redeem credibility, let's not assume that everyone has been doing it wrong all along. When everyone does it right for a little while, the burden will reduce.

'That which we persist in doing becomes easier – not that the nature of the task has changed, but our ability to do has increased.'

Ralph Waldo Emerson

25. Conclusion

We need change, but we need to change how we are changing. The entire script needs to be more positive, more proactive, more trusting and more responsible. Some of the solutions in the book should help us find our way out of our narrow definitions of conduct that give us a sense of security as they stop us from having our own independent view.

Realising our potential

The chaos theory refers to the science of surprises. Unlike traditional sciences that are linear and predictable (such as the law of gravity), the theory speaks of the non-linear and unpredictable, teaching us to expect the unexpected. It deals with things that are effectively impossible to predict or control, like turbulence, weather, the stock market, our brain states, and so on. Recognising that chaotic of this world can give us new insight. In the context of an organisation, there is no finite formula that will resolve all conduct issues. We are all a part of this chaos and we need to trust our instincts. Now combine this with The Secret as explained in Rhonda Byrne's book of that name. *The Secret*, also known as the law of attraction, is the idea that because of our connection with a universal energy force, our thoughts and feelings have the ability to manipulate this energy force to our liking attracting a corresponding energy to ourselves. Detrimental thoughts attract detrimental outcomes and vice-versa.

The essential message of *The Secret* is that we determine our destiny and create our reality. We need to be consistent and we get the corresponding output. Hence if we trust, we get corresponding outcomes. If we distrust, we still get corresponding outcomes. So before we resign to this chaos, we need to accept that it is our thoughts and feelings the power the future driving the non-linear and unpredictable – not only is it in our gift to influence this world, it is upon us to do so. That power is not a skill or an attitude that we need to acquire – it is us. We are that power. Collectively, can we not do more to take the conduct challenge in our hands and shape the story as we might like to see it?

For those of us who await the next big piece of news

to guide the organisation, we need to realise that we are the ones making those headlines – because it is our tiny interactions that set the tone of tomorrow's headlines. In the context of an organisation, those endless coffee chats, committee meetings, performance conversations, customer surveys, local forums, brainstorm sessions, project meetings, town halls, client dinners, lunch meetings, elevator pitches, recognition schemes, that pat on the back, that little nod, together, they determine the culture and direction of our organisation – we are the culture. There is power in the knowledge that the future is impossible to predict because it is yet to be written and we are the ones writing it.

Working together

Some of those involved in the crisis paid a hefty price, while some continued to thrive. But as with all crises, the masses suffered then and the masses suffer now as we deal with patchy, fragmented implementation remediation, we need to collaborate towards practical solutions that deliver for people at both ends of this spectrum – the one walking from the high streets into the banks and the ones walking from the banks into the streets. For when those bankers step on to the streets, they too become the ordinary people like the rest of us. When we take on jobs at the banks, we too become bankers. When the bankers switch to work for the regulator, they also become regulators, and when regulators work for the bank, they become bankers.

In trying to solve the issue of greed,

Let's not outcast them as another breed.

For they are plants of the same seed

Like us, a combination of good and bad deed

Economies will rise again and profits will return

Jobs will re-emerge, people will earn

But this question bothers me and I continue to yearn

As we rise from disaster, why don't we take time to learn?

Organisations need to take this as a lesson. A lesson not just to solve this one issue and keep up with regulation, but to keep looking out for problems and solve them – without making people feel like failures. Failure, as we know, is an event and never a person; and definitely not an entire industry!

Practising courageous leadership

There will always be risks and there will always be issues – if not from increased regulation then from reporting, systems, security, jurisdictions, economies. While I cannot be certain what the next issue will be, I can be certain that this isn't the last big issue we are dealing with. Whether we live in the rich world or in emerging economies, whether we are a bankers or a customer's – time and again, something will keep us awake at night. Globally, there will a relentless drive towards business optimisation; there will be challenges to raise productivity and continued pressure for increased investor returns. The key differentiators will be the ones who practise courageous leadership and create an environment of trust where people feel united in purpose and encouraged to explore. There will be little patience for those hiding behind committees where no decision is their own. It is the leader who needs to understand his business and the board that needs to ensure they have the right kind of leadership. Fewer committees and more decisions, less bureaucracy and more ownership. More courage.

Changing regulatory stance

As I started to write this book in May 2015, it constantly bothered me that the fear culture wasn't right and, as I continued to work through the book, Martin Wheatley was ousted from the FCA and I noted this article that summarised what I had been feeling throughout the course of writing. In the article Patrick Jenkins at the *Financial Times* reported that 'Politicians are not anti-finance any more: Eight years after the financial crisis, the political mood towards the financial services industry has softened ... removal of Mr. Wheatley was the biggest signal yet that the government is moving away from attack-dog regulation[xxxii]'.

I find regimental styles a bit regressive for where the world is today and where it will be tomorrow. If we stick to the understanding of conduct as forward looking and anticipating risk, the spirit is great and yet its application tedious and burdensome infused with high compliance costs and stringent penalties. I have discussed at length in this book through day-to-day examples how decisions that seem right to one, may seem wrong to another, right to me today may seem wrong to me tomorrow, so for that one in a million decision that was absolutely wrong from the start, how wise might it be to burden the other 9,99,999 decisions and expect the entire machinery to be able to survive the added load? We need to see decisions for what they are – efforts to lead a business in light of everything else and not sinister plans to harm the economy.

If anything, banks could be reassured that they will not be penalised as long as they meet certain requirements. We have seen banks withdraw from markets, leaving behind less competition and reduced choice; do we want the same of key resources in an environment already caught in fear and shortage of skills?

The Economist's' article 'One Regulator to Rule Them All' captured this quote from a former regulator. 'The best way to regulate is to line the banks up occasionally and shoot one of them.' [xxxiii] It bears a similarity to Donald Trump's attitude to Mexicans as he ran for the Republican nomination for President in the 2016 US elections, claiming that he wanted to build a wall on the Mexican border. It's all too convenient to round them all up. The article said that regulators were not the only ones with an interest in the stake. 'Investors in banks, insurers are financially exposed to the decisions of regulators. They have rights too. Systems ostensibly designed to ensure safety can easily backfire...'

Lifting standard and trust requires a more collaborative, dynamic work ethic, not looking at things firm by firm but as one global village where no part is unaffected by the actions of another. The entire conduct debate begs for more prudence.

Finding the key differentiator – your people

In the face of new technological forces, innovative competition, increased regulatory scrutiny, complex business structures, increasing reliance on global suppliers and third parties, organisations need people who can cut through it all with agility and passion. In this increasingly deregulated, global and digital economy, employees will be a key differentiator and skill retention will continue to be a challenge. Quoting from the Robert Walters half year 2015 report, there is a clear talent shortage as firms look for change professionals, be it compliance change, risk change, process change, etc. Of the businesses surveyed, 43 % felt that the skills shortage made it difficult for them to meet deadlines and client expectations. Another 24% said it affected staff morale, while 18% said it led to decreased productivity and high turnover. Key drivers of future requirement are regulatory reporting, remediation, and process improvements, among others.

Managing risk in the right context

Risk needs to be managed, but managing risk cannot be the purpose of existence; we exist for a purpose and manage risk around it, not vice-versa. While we cannot deny the need for good governance, risk management and an ethical culture, we first need a goal to strive towards – the rest is contextual. When we get out of bed in the morning, we don't wake up to manage the risks of living, we wake up to live our lives and manage risks so that we can live well. If it's sunny, we get sunscreen, if it's rainy, we get an umbrella and if we want to go on a holiday, we get insurance to secure our travel plans. If it all appears too risky, maybe goals need to be realigned. Risk must be managed in the most sustainable and holistic way possible, so that the risk management doesn't distract us from the pursuit of the goal. Firms need to assess whether they can really afford to have multiple risk units to slice and dice the same risk from multiple angles and offer expert opinion, or if they should divert resources to those who can offer solution rather than analysis; more doers than reporters, more action and less discussion.

Risk units may like to consider redefining their role from being the ones to protect the firm by flagging every possible risk, to those who support the firm in meeting its objectives, while ensuring that they keep it safe. I could totally protect my children by never allowing them to step out of the house, looking into options for home schooling and introducing multiple controls and limits, but that would just smother them and maybe even make them incompetent for the world they will face one day. As they grow, they need to venture and explore, make their share of mistakes, stumble, fall, rise, cry, fight, make up, continue to learn and discover who they are. My role is to help them find their purpose not to block their vision. There is such a thing as too much risk resilience, the tipping point at which organisations go from becoming risk aware to becoming risk averse, and that's when we see issues such as lack of innovation, a blame culture, slow decisions and generally low morale. Let's try not to go there.

Making it last

Do we want our conduct tune to be a hit single, here today and gone tomorrow, or do we want it to be something that plays through this challenge and the next, and the next.

If we want this to last, it can't be a bolt-on, it must be integrated like character into our existence, like yarn into the fabric. There are many ways to do this, but the simple ways are the most effective ones because, simple solutions stick.

1. Define what you want to achieve: Know what you stand for and make sure your people understand.
2. Know the price: Specify just how much risk you want them to take in pursuit of these objectives.
3. Worry about your business, and good conduct will follow: Shift your focus from conduct to your business and its conduct – the way you conduct your business in the context of your customers. As I see firms focus on conduct and get caught up in regulatory deadlines, I wonder why we get caught up in only the top-down approach and

forget the bottom-up and end-to-end, overlooking sloppy processes and recurring low-key items.

4. Earn credibility: Once we have defined what we want to achieve, we need to be consistent and stop changing our approach unless we have a good reason.

5. Good behaviour is not a task, but a way to be: We need to stop trying to be one-trick ponies trying to outshine everyone on a given day but find ways to be able to stand strong assessment after assessment; consistent and resilient, with less and less added effort as we get better at it.

We all reflect on each other individually and collectively, and often decisions could be at odds and there is no easy answer. However, therein lies our opportunity to speak up and be heard, to learn, to grow and to be more.

We need to listen carefully to the regulation and make a choice for pragmatism and progress; not to find that when faced with the needs to meet challenges, we had our heads stuck in the sands.

I'd like to end with a story. A scorpion and a frog needed to cross the river. As the scorpion sat on the frog's back, the frog asked if the scorpion if he would sting him. The scorpion said he needed to get to the other side alive so it was not in its interest to kill the frog. Half-way there, the scorpion stung the frog. The dying frog said, you said you wouldn't sting. Now we will both die. The scorpion said, how I could not? It's in my nature to sting.

Let's not be scorpions.

Acknowledgements

I would like to thank the following for all their help and support:

My parents, Mala Wadhwani and Neetha Paul for sticking with me through the course of the book.

Ashok Vaswani, Pete Horrell, Didier Vondaeniken, Anne Grim, Scott Graham and Kieran O'Meara for their trust and encouragement.

Lex van Dam, for support with content that resonates in spirit.

James Pao and Endre Urbancsok, for the daily dose of silly jokes, coffees and nachos – little things that kept me going strong.

Cherry Mosteshar, Henrietta Smethurst-McIntyre, and Dennis Hamley – the editorial team that made this book possible.

And above all, my children, Siya and Rocco, for putting up with me while the book consumed me, stalling trips to Legoland, and many more...

About the author:

Vinita Ramtri is the Head of Conduct Risk at Barclays Wealth. She regularly participates in industry-level meetings to influence thinking around conduct. In previous roles, she has handled change management and leadership training. She began her career with The Oberoi Hotels in India.

This is her first published book. She blogs with WeAreTheCity India (www.wearethecity.in), an online platform which supports the career development of Indian women. In 2015, she won the Rising Stars Award in the Investment Management category, an award recognising female talent pipeline.

You can follow Vinita on Twitter (@vinita_ramtri) or visit her at vinitaramtri.com.

Vinita lives with her two children in London.

In her spare time she loves to run, read, connect, and enjoy the little things in life.

References

i https://en.wikipedia.org/wiki/Inside_Job_(2010_film)
ii http://www.dailymail.co.uk/health/article-2655170/The-financial-crisis-caused-10-000-suicides-Europe-North-America-study-shows.html#ixzz3hf47NHir
iii https://www.fca.org.uk/about/history
iv https://www.fca.org.uk/your-fca/documents/fsa-journey-chapter-summaries
v http://www.bbc.co.uk/news/business-32198976
vi http://www.bbc.co.uk/news/uk-21335872
vii http://t.co/Y2cip4oD9N
viii http://t.co/fzetxzHiE1
ix http://www.telegraph.co.uk/finance/newsbysector/banksandfinance/11872971/HSBC-could-stay-in-UK-hints-chairman-Douglas-Flint.html
x http://www.bbc.co.uk/news/business-32618769
xi http://pwc.blogs.com/press_room/2015/06/pwclondon-business-school-research-reveals-why-bankers-cant-be-scared-into-doing-the-right-thing.html
xii http://www.cityam.com/219305/were-spending-billions-shopping-online-while-commuting
xiii Lex van Dam, 'How to make money trading', page 46
xiv http://www.horsesforsources.com/vishal-talks-to-phil_072415#sthash.FGhAaowc.dpuf
xv http://www.enca.com/south-africa/reformed-fraudster-help-curb-cybercrime
xvi https://www.gov.uk/government/news/no-more-paper-counterpart-to-the-photocard-driving-licence-will-save-the-taxpayer-millions-each-year
xvii http://www.telegraph.co.uk/news/worldnews/europe/italy/11271437/Schettino-I-was-number-one-on-the-Costa-Concordia-after-God.html
xviii http://www.thecityuk.com/research/our-work/reports-list/key-facts-about-uk-financial-and-related-professional-services/
xix Richard Rierson, Dose of leadership. Podcast 89. Speedoftrust.com
xx http://www.thisismoney.co.uk/money/news/article-3155239/CITY-INTERVIEW-Bureaucracy-bashing-Barclays-chairman-John-McFarlane-ousting-former-boss-Antony-Jenkins.html#ixzz3hdjeTFmM

[xxi] www.insights.barclays.co.uk

[xxii] http://citywire.co.uk/new-model-adviser/news/fca-fines-and-fees-counting-the-cost-of-regulation/a801659?re=33098&ea=379020&utm_source=BulkEmail_NMA_Weekly&utm_medium=BulkEmail_NMA_Weekly&utm_campaign=BulkEmail_NMA_Weekly#i=3

[xxiii] April 18th issues. Management editor and author of the report: Adrian Woolridge

[xxiv] http://www.bbc.co.uk/news/world-asia-31433736

[xxv] http://www.dailymail.co.uk/news/article-2381805/Warning-ahead-98-cent-drivers-understand-dashboard-lights.html#ixzz3cG7oVNdm

[xxvi] https://www.youtube.com/watch?v=YlGlTbr5DcQ

[xxvii] The Q1 2015 Emerging Risks Survey published by CEB (Corporate Executive Board Company)

[xxviii] Danny Shaw, BBC, 02 July 2015

[xxix] http://www.content-loop.com/big-dating-bringing-real-data-to-the-dating-game/

[xxx] http://www.fca.org.uk/news/fca-fines-rbs-natwest-and-ulster-bank-ltd-42m-for-it-failures

[xxxi] http://www.triz.co.uk/cp13.php?gclid=COSEiZ7s-sYCFajHtAodr0UOxQ

[xxxii] http://www.ft.com/cms/s/0/08ccabba-3229-11e5-8873-775ba7c2ea3d.html#axzz3nU3eiF5f

[xxxiii] http://www.economist.com/news/leaders/21660534-officials-have-been-given-enormous-discretion-corral-finance-has-costs-one-regulator

Made in the USA
Charleston, SC
24 November 2015